Bernie Madoff

by Don Nardo

LUCENT BOOKS

A part of Gale, Cengage Learning

GALE
CENGAGE Learning™

Detroit • New York • San Francisco • New Haven, Conn • Waterville, Maine • London

© 2011 Gale, Cengage Learning

LIBRARY OF CONGRESS CATALOGING-IN-PUBLICATION DATA

Nardo, Don, 1947-
  Bernie Madoff / by Don Nardo.
    p. cm. -- (People in the news)
  Includes bibliographical references and index.
  ISBN 978-1-4205-0353-1 (hbk.)
    1. Madoff, Bernard L.--Juvenile literature. 2. Swindlers and swindling--United States--Biography--Juvenile literature. 3. Ponzi schemes--United States--Juvenile literature. 4. Commercial crimes--United States--Juvenile literature. I. Title.
  HV6692.M33N37 2011
  364.16'3092--dc22
  [B]
                                                                    2010035237

Lucent Books
27500 Drake Rd.
Farmington Hills, MI 48331

ISBN-13: 978-1-4205-0353-1
ISBN-10: 1-4205-0353-7

Printed in the United States of America
1 2 3 4 5 6 7 15 14 13 12 11

Printed by Bang Printing, Brainerd, MN, 1st Ptg., 02/2011

Contents

F ame and celebrity are alluring. People are drawn to those who walk in fame's spotlight, whether they are known for great accomplishments or for notorious deeds. The lives of the famous pique public interest and attract attention, perhaps because their experiences seem in some ways so different from, yet in other ways so similar to, our own.

Newspapers, magazines, and television regularly capitalize on this fascination with celebrity by running profiles of famous people. For example, television programs such as *Entertainment Tonight* devote all of their programming to stories about entertainment and entertainers. Magazines such as *People* fill their pages with stories of the private lives of famous people. Even newspapers, newsmagazines, and television news frequently delve into the lives of well-known personalities. Despite the number of articles and programs, few provide more than a superficial glimpse at their subjects.

Lucent's People in the News series offers young readers a deeper look into the lives of today's newsmakers, the influences that have shaped them, and the impact they have had in their fields of endeavor and on other people's lives. The subjects of the series hail from many disciplines and walks of life. They include authors, musicians, athletes, political leaders, entertainers, entrepreneurs, and others who have made a mark on modern life and who, in many cases, will continue to do so for years to come.

These biographies are more than factual chronicles. Each book emphasizes the contributions, accomplishments, or deeds that have brought fame or notoriety to the individual and shows how that person has influenced modern life. Authors portray their subjects in a realistic, unsentimental light. For example, Bill Gates—the cofounder and chief executive officer of the software giant Microsoft—has been instrumental in making personal computers the most vital tool of the modern age. Few dispute his business savvy, his perseverance, or his technical expertise, yet critics say he is ruthless in his dealings with competitors and driven more by his desire to maintain Microsoft's dominance in the computer industry than by an interest in furthering technology.

In these books, young readers will encounter inspiring stories about real people who achieved success despite enormous obstacles. Oprah Winfrey—the most powerful, most watched, and wealthiest woman on television today—spent the first six years of her life in the care of her grandparents while her unwed mother sought work and a better life elsewhere. Her adolescence was colored by promiscuity, pregnancy at age fourteen, rape, and sexual abuse.

Each author documents and supports his or her work with an array of primary and secondary source quotations taken from diaries, letters, speeches, and interviews. All quotes are footnoted to show readers exactly how and where biographers derive their information and provide guidance for further research. The quotations enliven the text by giving readers eyewitness views of the life and accomplishments of each person covered in the People in the News series.

In addition, each book in the series includes photographs, annotated bibliographies, timelines, and comprehensive indexes. For both the casual reader and the student researcher, the People in the News series offers insight into the lives of today's newsmakers—people who shape the way we live, work, and play in the modern age.

A Matter of Trust

On a Monday evening in mid-December 2008, a sixty-five-year-old French financier named René-Thierry Magon de la Villehuchet went to his office in Manhattan, in New York City. (A financier is a person who routinely gets involved in large-scale business and investment deals.) There, he had long overseen a major link between the large financial markets located on New York's renowned Wall Street, and numerous wealthy French and other European investors.

Villehuchet looked backed with pride on his prominent and turbulent family history. The head of one of France's remaining aristocratic families, he often bragged to clients and acquaintances that twenty of his ancestors had been beheaded by the French mobs that had run amok during the famous French Revolution of 1789. As fate would have it, a smaller but no less sharp blade would soon end Villehuchet's own life. Satisfied that his employees had all gone home for the day, he locked the doors and went to his desk. Sitting down, he methodically removed a bottle of sleeping pills from his coat, took several, and then slashed his wrists with a box cutter.

Some of Villehuchet's employees discovered the bloody scene the next morning. At first they did not know what had prompted the tragic suicide. But it soon became clear that their boss had suddenly lost $1.4 billion dollars. Some of the money had been his own. But the bulk of the funds had belonged to his European clients, whose hard-earned money he had invested, hoping to get them the best financial returns possible.

Villehuchet was not the only person or group to have learned in the preceding week that he, she, or it had taken a major financial hit. Others included noted actor Kevin Bacon; movie director Steven Spielberg; Fred Wilpon, owner of the New York Mets; wealthy Boston businessman Carl Shapiro; the pension funds of numerous groups of teamsters and firefighters; several hospitals; Tufts and Yeshiva universities; the New York Law School; and the list went on and on, totaling close to five thousand individuals and organizations.

All on this fateful list had more in common than the loss of cripplingly large sums of money. A more important factor linking them was that they were all victims of the biggest investment fraud in history. The scam had been perpetrated by Bernie Madoff, a well-known and very rich New York–born stock and investment broker. For a very long time, he had enjoyed a stellar reputation. In addition to being famous on Wall Street as one of its most active and

Madoff investor René-Thierry Magnon de la Villehuchet committed suicide in his office after losing $1.4 billion in Madoff's investment scheme.

honest traders, he had also supported numerous charities over the years. Yet these seemingly aboveboard activities turned out to be a smoke screen for highly shady dealings. As another of Madoff's victims, Bert Ross, former mayor of Fort Lee, New Jersey, puts it:

> Bernie Madoff is a scam artist. . . . Being on boards of charities and giving to charity—everything he did was to cloak himself with the air of respectability. [Famous English novelist Charles] Dickens couldn't come up with a better name for this guy—Madoff. He made off with everybody's money.[1]

Too Good to Be True?

Ross and the other victims had also put full trust in Madoff, never realizing until too late that their trust had been horribly misplaced. Certainly they had not been the first investors to trust their brokers. For many centuries, but especially in the past century or so, people looking for ways to make their money grow and multiply sought reliable ways to invest it. The vast majority of them lacked the expertise about the stock market and other investment arenas to make the appropriate deals themselves. So they turned to experienced brokers. Such experts were said to know the ins and outs of investing money so that it would grow over time.

Not surprisingly, therefore, many interested investors sought out Madoff, who was one of the most successful of all the financial managers and brokers of the twentieth century. He had begun his Wall Street firm—Bernard L. Madoff Investment Securities—in the 1960s, when still a young man. Steadily but surely, over the course of more than three decades, he had expanded the company. At the same time, he had gained a reputation almost second to none in the industry. People and organizations across the country and in several foreign nations, too, had consistently heard that Madoff knew his stuff. According to the financial grapevine, made up of well-off investors of all walks of life, he had a phenomenal knack for knowing where to invest his clients' money. In short, he could be counted on to earn them big dividends (profits). Relatives told relatives, and friends told friends about their good fortune in hooking up with this apparent financial wizard. That translated into a long line of potential investors waiting to hand over their earnings—often their entire life savings—to Madoff.

But most of these eager, satisfied investors did not pay enough heed to an old adage that has consistently stood the test of time. Namely, if something seems too good to be true, it probably is. History has shown that the best financial brokers in the business are unable to reap huge profits all, or even most, of the time. The fact that Madoff always seemed to be able to find lucrative deals for his customers, no matter how bad the market was doing at the time, should have been a red flag for those customers.

The truth was that Madoff's financial empire had been erected atop faulty foundations. In the corridors of Wall Street and other moneymaking institutions across the world, some experts instinctively doubted that Madoff could be 100 percent legitimate. In their view, he did not pass the so-called smell test. But few openly questioned him, and his client list continued to grow.

The Enormity of the Scheme

Finally, however, Madoff's company collapsed of its own weight. Incredibly, it turned out, he had not been investing his clients' funds at all, as everyone assumed he had been. Instead, he had been banking and/or spending the money. Even more incredible and disturbing was the fact that Madoff had realized for years that he would not be able to get away with his fraud indefinitely. He later told the court that convicted him:

> When I began my [financial] scheme, I believed it would end shortly and I would be able to extricate [free] myself and my clients from the scheme. . . . I always knew this day would come. I never invested the money. I deposited it into a Chase Manhattan Bank.[2]

Indeed, the amount of money that Madoff collected but deposited rather than invested ran into the billions—$50 billion in all. To make the enormity of this criminal scheme clearer, one of Madoff's biographers places this fantastically high figure in some more recognizable contexts:

DAILY NEWS

75¢   **2.5 MILLION READERS EVERY DAY**   NYDailyNews.com

WHAT BERNIE MADE OFF WITH

THE FULL AMAZING LIST PAGES 6-7

Reviled Madoffs own more than 826M in planes, homes & assets

Rihanna's back in town

PAGE 5

The New York Daily News's March 14, 2009, issue poked fun at Madoff's name while revealing the enormous amount of wealth he had accumulated.

Fifty billion is about $163 for each of the 305 million people estimated to be living in the U.S. in [the month Madoff was arrested—December 2008]. Fifty billion is more than all but six U.S. states spend each year. Fifty billion is more than the annual budgets of the U.S. Departments of Labor, Interior, Transportation, Treasury, and NASA, combined.[3]

That the amount of money Madoff successfully stole from his clients was so enormous can be attributed only to the equally huge amount of trust they placed in him and in the financial system in which he worked. For a variety of reasons, Madoff's clients had thoroughly trusted him and the large-scale investment system with their money. But both the system and the man had turned out not to be worthy of that trust. As well-known financier Leon Levy pointed out in 2002, in the decades immediately preceding that year, the Wall Street scene had become riddled with brokers, company managers, and others who were driven in large part by greed. Not all broke the law to satisfy that greed. But many insiders engaged in practices that maximized their personal profits at the expense of outsiders—clients who desired to exploit the stock market but knew little about how it works.

At the same time, Levy and other experts say, a few of the most knowledgeable insiders, such as Madoff, had been willing to cross the line and engage in illegal practices to further their own aims. In so doing, they have made the system an even less trustworthy place in which to do business. Indeed, Levy says, along with the money people stood to lose as a result of shady practices was "the crucial element of trust." The lesson that members of the public can learn, he adds, is that

> neither companies nor the analysts [financial experts] supposedly assessing those companies' prospects can be trusted. Nor can people always trust the independent accountants who certify company reports. They cannot even always trust the financial cops of the Securities and Exchange Commission to catch cheaters in a timely fashion.[4]

In retrospect, Madoff clearly took full advantage of this financial system in which complete trust had become an increasingly rare commodity. He used every method and trick he could to build up his clients' trust, both in that system and in himself as a key player within it. Ultimately, he betrayed that trust, in the process ruining the lives of thousands of people. The story of Madoff's rise and fall is therefore, among other things, a cautionary reminder about the risks of relying too much on someone else's honesty and integrity. It is a classic, tragic tale of human trust extended in good faith and then in bad faith exploited and broken, primarily in the name of personal greed.

Chapter 1

Happy Days on Rockaway Beach

Not much of a substantial nature is known about the early life of the man who eventually came to be known both as the biggest crook in America and the country's most hated man. Indeed, records of Madoff's childhood are fairly scarce. Also, what little is known about his earliest years indicates that nothing was particularly memorable about him. Indeed, according to people who grew up with and still remember him, as a child he showed little beyond the ordinary in his intelligence, creative talents, or anything else. For example, fellow high school swim team member Fletcher Eberle later recalled:

> The Bernie I knew was a good-natured, happy-go-lucky guy, always smiling and kidding, who swam the butterfly very well and never got overly serious. If you had said to me that Bernie was going to be chairman of the Nasdaq [the famous electronic board that lists stock market prices] and make all this money, I never would have believed it possible.[5]

Nevertheless, in retrospect a few incidents from Madoff's largely lackluster childhood seem to hint at the selfish, devious individual he would become as an adult.

Familiar Family Stories

Madoff's family background was no less unremarkable and sparsely documented as his own early life. Indeed, the stories of his grandparents and parents are in several ways similar to those of millions of immigrants who came to the United States seeking better lives in the early years of the twentieth century. Both Bernie's father, Ralph Madoff, and mother, Sylvia Muntner Madoff came from Eastern European Jewish families. Both sets of grandparents fled Poland and Romania shortly before World War I (1914–1918) to escape intense anti-Jewish purges in those lands. Along with many other immigrants from Europe and other regions, they landed along with their young children in New York City. There, they began making new lives for themselves in the "land of the free," as the United States was, and still is, often called.

Ralph and Sylvia met in New York City in 1932, in the early stages of the Great Depression. That huge financial downturn—the worst in modern history—had resulted in large part from the 1929 collapse of the U.S. stock market centered on Wall Street in New York. Hauntingly, Wall Street and the market would continue to loom as major presences in the family's background. Nearly every person in the Madoff family would end up working in or investing heavily in the stock market. Most prominent of all, of course, would be Bernie Madoff, whose name would become synonymous with the corruption, excess, and greed so often associated with large financial markets and dealings.

Bernie was born on April 29, 1938, in the New York City borough of Queens. At the time, he had a four-year-old sister named Sondra. A younger brother, Peter, was born sometime between 1941 and 1945. Both before and after these births, Ralph Madoff moved his family from one city borough to another, spending some time in Brooklyn and the Bronx as well as Queens. Throughout the period, he worked in a number of jobs, including plumber and assistant manager of a jewelry store. But his dream was to become a successful player in the stock market.

Sandlot Baseball and Amusement Parks

Finally, in 1946, shortly after the end of World War II, the family settled in the small town of Laurelton, near Rockaway Beach, both in southern Queens. Laurelton is situated some 16 miles (26km) southeast of downtown Manhattan. The most famous of New York City's boroughs, Manhattan is home to Wall Street and the stock market, where Bernie's financial empire would later rise and fall.

Today, with all sorts of public transportation available, Laurelton and Rockaway Beach do not seem very distant from Manhattan. But in the 1940s and 1950s, Laurelton did not have its own subway stop. So, outside of taking slow buses, it was not easy for local residents to connect with other New York boroughs. As a result, Laurelton long remained a small, quiet, somewhat sheltered community, existing seemingly far from what the Madoffs and their neighbors viewed as the mad scramble of the big city.

In 1946 the Madoff family moved to Laurelton, near Rockaway Beach, in southern Queens.

At Home in the Water

Although Bernie Madoff made no waves academically while in high school, he did manage to acquire a small name for himself in athletics. According to his boyhood friend Jay Portnoy:

> Bernie joined the Far Rockaway swimming team—the Mermen—as a sophomore. Since most of the meets were held right after school, several of us stayed after class to watch him compete. He usually swam the medley relay, doing either the butterfly or breast stroke. I recently found a 1954 issue of the Far Rockaway newsletter, the *Chat*. It mentioned that the Mermen finished their season with a 4-4 record, but also noted that Bernie's medley team had won their last two contests. He later used his swimming skills to secure a summer job as a lifeguard with the NYC Parks Department on the Rockaway beaches.

Jay Portnoy, "Growing Up with the Ponzi King," *Saratogian*, February 13, 2009. www
.saratogian.com/articles/2009/02/13/news/doc49959c85cb664044256888.txt.

Exactly what Bernie Madoff did in that sheltered community in his grade school years is uncertain. Probably, says financial researcher Peter Sander, who wrote a book about Madoff's rise from obscurity, the young man took advantage of the opportunities available to other local boys his age. These included playing

> street and sandlot baseball and [swimming] in the Atlantic Ocean in the summer. And that's likely what Madoff spent most of his time doing, while probably idolizing the Brooklyn Dodgers and dreaming of becoming a baseball star like most kids did in the area [in] the 1940s and 1950s. . . . Special treats might have involved trips to the local Rockland Playland [an amusement park]. More ambitious journeys may have taken him to Coney Island [a

peninsula in southern Brooklyn known for its many beaches, amusement parks, and fast-food vendors].[6]

Early Social Relationships

It appears that young Bernie's school activities were, for the most part, as average as his out-of-school ones. His childhood friend Jay Portnoy recalls the grade school the two attended—PS 156:

[It] was a three-story, 9 A.M. to 3 P.M., eight-grade elementary school. Bernie and I graduated in June of '52. There were five sections to each class from the 6th grade to the 8th. In 6th grade we shared gym and music-appreciation classes, and we were together in 8th, sharing teachers for English, science, mathematics, and more, at different times. Each hour we would march along the third-floor hall walls counter-clockwise to our next class.[7]

While they attended PS 156, Portnoy remembers, his friend already had begun to show a tendency to use other people to further his own aims. At that time, young Bernie was the cofounder of a social club called the Ravens, the members of which wore sweaters with small raven insignias sewn on. "They were the status organization for my age group," Portnoy explains.

There was a counter-club . . . called the Macabees, [of which] I was one of its earlier members. Both clubs met in the Laurelton Jewish Center, across the street from PS 156. The Macabees was nearly completely Jewish in composition. The Ravens were pretty much split between Jews and Gentiles [non-Jews]. In the fall of 1951, I was invited to join the Ravens. I eagerly accepted since I was somewhat surprised that I was wanted. The Ravens had a reverse quota system. Since they were housed in a Jewish synagogue, [they] always had one more Jew than non-Jews. This way they could justify their presence as a Jewish organization. If a popular Gentile was wanted as a member, they had to search for a usually-less popular Jew to invite. Only decades later did I realize that this was probably the cause for my unexpected recruitment.[8]

Looking back on their school experiences, Portnoy and other Madoff classmates wonder whether Bernie's promotion of the Ravens was an attempt to divert attention from his second-rate academic performances. "I don't remember Bernie being that bright at all,"[9] fellow student Elsa Levine (then Elsa Lipson), recalls. Another young woman attending PS-156, Marcia Mendelsohn, who spent a lot of time with Bernie in eighth grade, agreed. "I remember he was always disappointed getting his grades," she writes, "because he didn't make the honor society. He wanted to be in the honor classes. We all knew. He was always the struggler." Moreover, she adds, "he had an inferiority complex. He never felt he was good enough."[10]

High School Days

Bernie's disappointing grades continued in his last four years of schooling. He went to Far Rockaway High School, an imposing old building attended by students from Laurelton and a few other nearby small towns. By this time, in the early-to-mid 1950s, the school and the communities it served were part of a distinctly old-fashioned, innocent social lifestyle and atmosphere that would be fondly recreated decades later in various TV shows and movies. "Think *Happy Days*,"[11] one modern observer says. Nora Koeppel, who attended Far Rockaway High School in the same years Bernie did, concurs, saying:

> In those years, even at the age of twelve, you could catch a bus on Rockaway Beach Boulevard, which would take you to . . . the movies at the Strand or Columbia Theater or to the bowling alley, which was above the stores. Of course, the day also consisted of going to the Pickwick luncheonette for a snack. The Rockaways were always safe and fun.[12]

Movies, bowling, and fast food cost money, of course. Madoff managed to make the spending money he needed for these activities partly by working as a lifeguard at local beaches. He also

Ruth Alpern appears in the 1958 Far Rockaway High School yearbook. She met Madoff in his senior year.

installed lawn sprinklers in Laurelton during the summer months. Exactly how much he made doing this is unknown. In later years, he claimed this is how he saved enough money to start his financial investments business after college. However, his adult life eventually became so filled with half-truths and outright lies that it is hard to know if this was actually the case.

Indeed, one high school incident, perhaps among several, demonstrated that young Bernie was neither unwilling nor afraid to try to cheat the system and con people. Portnoy later recalled how his friend managed to get away with delivering a blatantly phony book report in English class:

> We were scheduled to make oral book reports. Prior to the presentations, Bernie had looked at my book and pro-nounced it "boring." "Hardly any pictures," he proclaimed.

He was among the first to do his report; but he had not yet read any book. Not visibly concerned, he announced his title as *Hunting and Fishing* by Peter Gunn [the name of a fictional detective in a 1950s TV show]. . . . Bernie glided through his book report, excusing the material lack of the book by reporting its return to the public library. [I don't know if] the teacher saw through [the ruse or not].[13]

Not everyone who cheats on a school assignment goes on to become a criminal, of course. However, Bernie Madoff did exactly that. Decades later, a large number of people would end up financially supporting a scheme of his that was no more real than that high school book report.

After High School

It was in his senior year of high school that Madoff met and fell for Ruth Alpern, who was two years younger than he was. Various classmates described her as a pretty blonde with green eyes who dressed smartly in plaid skirts and button-down shirts. "Bernie had found his biggest fan and future wife," biographer Andrew Kirtzman remarks. "Ruthie saw a spark in him that others did not. She believed in him when others hadn't. They became each other's best friend and closest confidant and stayed joined at the hip for decades to come. It would be a half-century before events would pull them apart."[14]

Because they admired each other so much, Madoff regularly stayed in touch with Ruth after he went off to college following his high school graduation in 1956. First he entered the University of Alabama, where his major, if any, remains unclear. Still an unremarkable, fairly disinterested student, he left after only a year and went back to New York. There, he attended what was then known as Hofstra College, on Long Island not too far from where he had grown up. His major was political science, although no evidence exists suggesting he had any special interest in that subject.

In November 1959, about a year before graduating from Hofstra, Madoff, then twenty-one, married his sweetheart, Alpern.

Ruth Looks Back with Pride

Ruth Alpern, who became Ruth Madoff in 1959, was proud of her husband and their life together. This is reflected in her remarks in the memorial booklet for her fiftieth high school reunion in 2008 (a mere month before Bernie Madoff was arrested for fraud):

> I graduated from Queens College in 1961. [My husband Bernie and I] worked together in the investment business he founded. We have 2 sons, 5 grandchildren. After spending some years in the family business, I went back to school to study nutrition and received a masters from NYU. During that time I co-authored *Great Chefs*, only available on eBay these days. I travel and hang out with my grandchildren. I'm on the board of Queens College, and the Gift of Life Bone Marrow foundation.

Quoted in Erin Arvedlund, *Too Good to Be True: The Rise and Fall of Bernie Madoff.* New York: Penguin, 2009, p. 22.

A photograph of Ruth and Bernie Madoff appears in the catalog from the fifty-year year reunion of the 1958 class of Far Rockaway High School.

They tied the knot at the Laurelton Jewish Center, where both had long had friends and acquaintances. Right afterward, they moved into a small one-bedroom apartment in Bayside, Queens.

Despite the fact that Madoff had already decided to try his hand working in the stock market, he remained in school and received his degreee the following October (1960). Less than a month later, he started his financial securities business, which was destined to make him rich and widely envied. No one could have guessed that this twenty-two-year-old man would also eventually become destitute and widely despised. Yet at least a few red flags had been laid down for future investigators to dig for and uncover. As Portnoy later said: "In retrospect, I wonder if I could have predicted Bernie's misdeeds from the decades [in which] I observed [him]. [All I can say is that as a boy] he showed pride of appearance, willingness to deceive, [and] no fear of the eventual consequences when there was a good chance of success."[15]

Chapter 2

The Good Bernie Madoff

Two different Madoff financial operations and, in a sense, two different Bernie Madoffs existed almost from the beginning. Initially, in 1960 Madoff started a standard stock-brokering, or stock-trading, firm. As a stock broker, or trader, the good Bernie Madoff, so to speak, bought and sold shares of stock from various companies for customers who paid him a commission, or fee, for doing so. Such trades are short-term deals in which the broker may or may not know the customer personally. Evidence suggests that that part of Madoff's business was and long remained aboveboard. It was the other and largely secretive part of the business that eventually proved to be corrupt. The bad Bernie Madoff took large sums of money from clients; he promised to invest the funds but never did.

What seems odd to many people in retrospect is why the bad Bernie Madoff emerged at all. The truth is that the good one did quite well with his brokering-trading business. In fact, over the years, the largely honest sector of Bernard L. Madoff Investment Securities made him rich and famous, at least in Wall Street circles. Therefore, why did Madoff resort to dishonesty? As biographer Erin Arvedlund points out:

> Bernie Madoff didn't need to be a crook. This was one of the things that most stunned Wall Street when the truth came to light. . . . In the world of stockbrokers, Bernie Madoff was a real, legitimate, big-league player. He and his brother had built

from scratch one of the most successful broker-dealer firms in New York. [People] in the business, those who needed fast, inexpensive stock trading, knew just where to go. Bernie Madoff was the man. He grew to be rich and powerful and highly respected in many circles. He didn't need to resort to crime to be successful. So why did he do it? Looking back, we can compare him to a World Series–winning baseball slugger taking steroids—he didn't need to do it, but it helped.[16]

Thus, Madoff's legitimate, genuine trading firm always existed alongside, and diverted attention from, his secret fraudulent operation. As a result, to get a full picture of his personality and life, both sides of the business and the man must be examined. A look at the honest, upfront business he built, nurtured over the years, and took considerable pride in reveals the side of Madoff that he likely felt was dominant. Certainly this was the side he wanted to project to family, friends, and the world.

The Hardworking Son-in-Law

The exact manner in which Madoff's stock-trading business came into being in 1960 remains somewhat unclear. He later claimed that he had saved up five thousand dollars from working as a lifeguard and sprinkler installer in the prior few years. Although that was no small sum in those days, it was not enough to set up a successful business in finance. So Madoff needed to borrow more money. Later, he admitted that he acquired a fifty-thousand-dollar loan from his father-in-law, Saul Alpern, a successful accountant.

Alpern was from the start highly impressed with his daughter's husband and appears to have believed strongly that Madoff would do well as a stockbroker. For that reason, Alpern provided further aid by referring some of his own friends and clients to his new son-in-law. If they wanted to buy and sell a few stocks, Alpern said, he knew a hardworking young man named Bernie Madoff who would gladly take care of them.

A third way that Saul Alpern helped out his daughter and her enterprising husband was by allowing them to use desk space

Like Parents Like Son?

Bernie Madoff was not the only person in his family who was fascinated with and desired to work in the stock market. In 1960, at about the same time he was starting up his stock-trading business, his parents, Ralph and Sylvia Madoff, began their own trading firm. They called it Gibraltar Securities. A number of friends, as well as people who worked in the stock market, thought it strange that the Madoffs ran their business out of their home in northern Queens. Little is known about Gibraltar, except that the SEC investigated it in 1963 along with some other small "mom and pop" stock-trading outfits. The Madoffs were cited for failing to file reports about their financial condition, and they closed down the business early in 1964 under circumstances that remain somewhat mysterious.

in his accounting offices. There, Bernie made deals over the phone, although sometimes he visited customers in person. Meanwhile, Ruth acted as the tiny company's bookkeeper.

Young Madoff worked hard at buying and selling stocks for his customers. Initially, he was what people in the financial trades called a wholesaler. He dealt in over-the-counter stocks, consisting mainly of shares in small companies that did not trade on the main floor of the stock exchanges in New York. Often he would get a call from another small dealer who lived and worked in a town or small city somewhere else in the country. That dealer would have a client who wanted to buy or sell shares in a certain company and had heard that Madoff could get the best per-share price for the stock in question. In return for brokering the deal, Madoff received a small fee from the dealer who had called (who also took a cut for himself). The same procedure also frequently happened in reverse. Sometimes Madoff would have a client who wanted to buy or sell some stock, and he felt he could get the best deal by phoning another small-time stockbroker like himself. Madoff later recalled:

This Third Avenue building in New York City contained the offices of Madoff Investment Securities. It was here that Madoff began using his payment for order flow investment schemes.

In those days, over-the-counter stocks were traded always over the telephone with no automation. So you would call a broker; the broker would call up over the telephone any number of dealers like myself, and there were hundreds of dealers around the country that were making [trading in] these markets.[17]

Phenomenal Growth

It soon became clear to Madoff that the more orders, or requests, he could get from other traders for such deals, the more money he could make. In other words, though each deal was typically small and paid little, he could make up for that by having a larger volume of deals. To that end, he began using a method known as "payment for order flow." Essentially, it was a small

Failing to Pass the Sniff Test

Not long after Madoff's arrest in 2008, the editor of the online financial review *Clusterstock*, John Carney, questioned Madoff's claim about making his business seed money of five thousand dollars by doing part-time jobs:

> One of the most basic parts of the Bernie Madoff story seems very dubious. According to the widely circulated legend, Madoff founded his [stock-trading firm] with $5000 he earned working part time as a lifeguard and installing sprinkler systems. . . . This particular story is implausible. While a college student might be able to save $5000 now by working summer jobs or doing part time home improvement work, there's almost no way that could be done in 1960. . . . Back then that was a lot of money. Adjusted for inflation, it was the equivalent of $35,000 today. To look at it differently, the median income in the US in 1960 was just $5,600. The idea that Madoff made this much working part time jobs while going to college doesn't pass the sniff test. [So] where did his money come from? Why did he feel like he needed to lie about it? These are questions that we hope investigators are asking.

John Carney, "Where Did Madoff's Startup Money Come From?" *Clusterstock*, December 22, 2008. www.businessinsider.com/2008/12/where-did-madoffs-startup-money-come-from.

kickback he paid to any third party—another broker, large or small—in return for throwing him some business. He did not invent the idea. But he was one of the first small-time brokers to use it often and consistently.

Some brokers and others in the financial industry frowned on payment for order flow. Though it was legal, they felt it was not in the best interest of the customer. As one expert explains, "Instead of routing [directing] orders to the dealer or to the outstanding order representing the best price, the order is routed to the dealer paying the kickback. So the customer doesn't get the best price [available for the stock]."[18] Various academic and other studies were made of the payment for order flow process in the 1970s and 1980s. For the most part, they took a neutral stance on the subject. Finally, in the early 1990s the Securities and Exchange Commission (SEC), the government agency that regulates the financial industry, decided not to ban the practice. That allowed Madoff to continue employing it.

More important, over the years Madoff had acquired many thousands of deals, some quite lucrative, by using payment for order flow. As a result, his legitimate stock-brokering business did better and better. In 1967 he was able to report more than $127,000 in earnings to the SEC, a lot of money for a small-scale broker at the time. Two years later, he made more than $555,000, and in 1973 the stock-trading portion of Bernard L. Madoff Investment Securities made $1.1 million. This phenomenal growth continued apace. By 1989 Madoff's company was handling up to 5 million shares of stock—fully 2 percent of the entire volume of the New York Stock Exchange—each and every day.

Rapid Automation

Another sign of Madoff's success was that he became a member of the National Association of Securities Dealers (NASD), a widely respected, self-regulated Wall Street organization. At one time or another, he served on both the board of directors and board of governors of the NASD. The connections he made while serving with that group helped lead Madoff to perhaps his greatest single triumph as an honest stockbroker. This was his participation in the development of consolidated (merged) and automated stock-trading systems that revolutionized the world's stock markets and other financial industries.

First, Madoff was a member of a special NASD committee that designed the Intermarket Trading System, or ITS. This was a new system that linked the many small, local stock exchanges across the country to the larger ones in New York City. The relatively small Boston Stock Exchange and San Francisco Stock Exchange, for instance, could now link up with the much bigger New York Stock Exchange (NYSE) and American Stock Exchange (AMEX). The latter two had long held a sort of monopoly on stocks of major companies. But the SEC wanted to make those, and in fact all, stocks more open to buyers and sellers in all markets. So it welcomed this large-scale consolidation of markets.

The key to making the new system work was computers. Then an imperfect but rapidly developing new electronic tool, the computer made possible the merging of dozens, even hundreds, of separate markets without the need for large numbers of workers exchanging information by hand, telegraph, or telephone. In fact, Madoff and his lawyer brother, Peter, who joined Bernard L. Madoff Investment Securities in about 1970, were among a select group of market pioneers who recognized the potential of computers to help run Wall Street. As the 1970s progressed, the Madoffs steadily computerized their own business, making stock trading and other activities much faster. They also urged others in the business to introduce such automation, which led to the formation of the ITS.

The ultimate result of this trend toward computerization and faster, more efficient trading was the success of the NASDAQ, which originally stood for National Association of Securities Dealers Automated Quotations. The world's first electronic stock market, it started out in 1971 as a fairly simple computer bulletin board that merely listed stock prices. Initially, it did not connect buyers and sellers. Nor did it negotiate trades and other deals. Over the years, however, the NASDAQ became increasingly sophisticated. As Wall Street watchers James Bandler and Nicholas Varchaver explain, the NASDAQ went through various stages of automation, so that you were able to turn on your computer screen and any brokerage firm in the country would list all the dealers that were willing to trade the security [stock] and the prices. Then that eventually went on to where you could actually trade the security automatically.[19]

NASDAQ started in 1971 as a simple computer board listing stock prices and evolved into connecting buyers and sellers and negotiating trade and other financial deals.

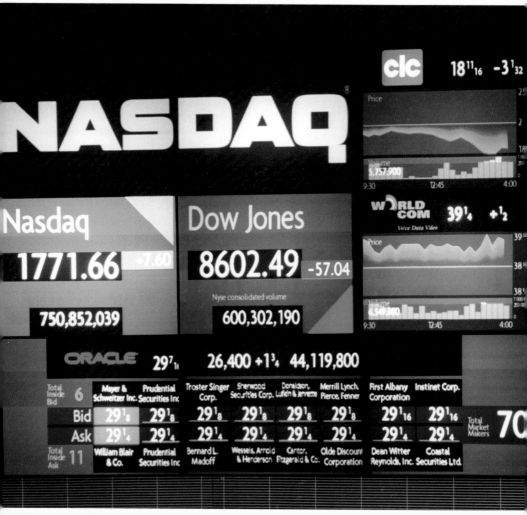

Reaping the Benefits

Although Madoff himself did not invent the NASDAQ, as some recent writers have mistakenly claimed, he did have a hand in its creation. So it is not surprising that he also shared handily in its success, which was rapid, even stunning. By 1981, just ten years after its emergence, the NASDAQ listed the stocks of more than three thousand companies, compared to some twenty-five hundred companies on the NYSE and AMEX combined. His own firm already completely computerized, Madoff reaped the benefits of the swift advance of automation throughout the Wall Street realm. According to one of his biographers, Andrew Kirtzman:

In the Days of Pink Sheets

When Madoff's stock-trading business began in the 1960s, before electronic markets like NASDAQ appeared, small-time brokers like himself used what the industry called "pink sheets," explained here by one of Madoff's biographers, Peter Sander.

> The pink sheets were—well—pink sheets of paper listing quotations for stocks from dealers. Each quotation would list the dealer's name, the stock, and a bid and ask price. The bid price was the price the dealer would pay for the shares you own. The ask, or "offer" price, was the price they would sell you shares for. . . . The difference or spread, represented the profit (the retail markup) the dealer would make on the security [stock]. Pink sheets were printed daily by the National Quotation Bureau [a private company that provided products and services to the various stock exchanges].

Peter Sander, *Madoff: Corruption, Deceit, and the Making of the World's Most Notorious Ponzi Scheme.* Guilford, CT: Lyons, 2009, p. 40.

With a more efficient marketplace, people began to take over-the-counter stocks [which had in prior decades been on the outer margins of the market] more seriously, and Madoff's business hit the big time. . . . Years later, the people he grew up with would scratch their heads over how such an average intellect could attain such heights. It turned out that Bernie Madoff had remarkable gifts, ones that emerged only when he entered the world of finance. His public success on Wall Street bestowed legitimacy on his operation and won him widespread respect. The kid who found his worth in business, selling sprinklers, once again won respect by making money.[20]

What people did not know at the time was that this legitimate Bernie Madoff was all the while being shadowed by the dishonest Bernie Madoff. Discreetly hidden behind closed doors, the latter was already up to no good.

and desk space in the Alpern accounting offices. Alpern also recommended some of his own clients and friends as possible investors. The assumption was that they would hand over lump sums of money to Madoff, who would find ways to invest the funds and make them grow over time. Like everyone else involved, Alpern was duped as well. All available evidence shows that he had no idea that his son-in-law, whom he greatly admired, was not on the up-and-up.

At first, a large proportion of Madoff's investors were fellow Jews who summered in the Catskills, a picturesque hilly region in south-central New York State. A number of old-style resort hotels there attracted people from New York City and other nearby urban areas who wanted to get away from the hustle and bustle of the city for at least a few months each year. As it happened, several of those who stayed at one of the more popular of these hotels, Sunny Oaks in Woodridge, New York, had something in common. Namely, they shared the same accountant— Saul Alpern. The vast majority of these vacationers were not wealthy. But most had managed to save moderate nest eggs for their retirements and were open to the idea of making those funds grow if the right opportunity materialized.

Just such an opportunity presented itself when Alpern told them that his brilliant, hardworking son-in-law would be glad to invest their money for them. Alpern initially collected between five thousand and fifty thousand dollars each from about twelve to fifteen of his clients and passed these monies on to Madoff. This was only the beginning of the latter's acquisition of a growing stable of victims. In the mid-1960s, with his accounting business doing well, Alpern decided to expand. He hired two extra accountants, Frank Avellino and Michael Bienes, who were about Madoff's age. Soon they, too, were referring clients to Madoff. Typically, they promised these would-be investors that they would make 13.5 to 20 percent profits on their seed money. This was and still is considered an unusual and suspiciously large amount of profit to be made on a regular, continuous basis. In all, Alpern, Avellino, and Bienes funneled at least half a billion dollars' worth of business to Madoff over the course of three decades.

"He Had Me"

In an April 2009 article for *Fortune* magazine, investigators James Bandler and Nicholas Varchaver report how Madoff lured in clients through the power of his seemingly soft-spoken, friendly personality and ability to make others feel like family:

> [Accountant and Madoff associate Michael] Bienes re-calls [that] Madoff invited him to the bar mitzvah of one of his sons. "It was a lunch," Bienes recalls, "a buffet lunch. And I was very impressed because he didn't go over the top. He was a wealthy guy, you know, but he did it in a very moderate way. And I remember my partner, Frank Avellino, and myself and Bernie meeting in the middle of the dance floor, and we were saying, 'Thanks for having us,' and he said, 'Hey, come on. We're family, aren't we?' And at that moment, he had me. He had me. We were family. Oh, my God! I was in! It really took me because he had a presence about him, an aura. He really captivated you." Bienes, who ulti-mately lost his entire savings to Madoff, still seems daz-zled decades later.

Quoted in James Bandler and Nicholas Varchaver, "How Bernie Did It," *Fortune*, April 30, 2009. http://money.cnn.com/2009/04/24/news/newsmakers/madoff.fortune/index .htm?postversion=2009042406.

James Bandler, (left), and Nicholas Varchaver received the Loeb Award for Distin-guished Business and Financial Journalism in 2010 for their story in Fortune *magazine about the Madoff investment scheme.*

Although the three accountants thought Madoff was an honest financial manager, they were not totally blameless in helping him. They were licensed as accountants, not as money managers or investment advisers. Thus, in collecting investment funds from clients for Madoff, they were acting illegally, which would get them into trouble later.

Nevertheless, they were also victims of Madoff's scheme. Like other family and friends, they invested their own funds with him. Bienes later wrote: "One of the first things Alpern said to me when I went to work for him was: 'Listen, you got money, you can invest it with my son-in-law, Bernie. You'll get 20 percent.'" At first, Bienes felt he did not have enough to invest. But "a few short years later," he recalled, "my wife had saved up $5,000, and she says, 'I want to open an account with Bernie.' And he let her do it. And she started with $5,000."[22]

What Have You Got to Lose?

This anecdote is an example of how Madoff long managed to expand and perpetrate his fraud almost solely through word of mouth. Indeed, until the 1980s and 1990s, nearly every person he conned heard about his money-managing business from a friend or family member. Early investors were so happy with Madoff that, in the words of one expert, they were "converted into an instant sales force"[23] for him.

These clients came to make up what was in a sense a private club, one in which new members were few and well-screened by Madoff himself. In fact, he purposely made it seem as if he was reluctant to admit new investors unless they understood and agreed to certain ground rules. The most important of these was secrecy. As part of the con, he pushed the idea that he was so good at what he did that it was an enormous privilege to invest with him. In order to benefit from that singular privilege, investors were expected to keep details of their financial relationships with him confidential. Not surprisingly, most of his investors had no problem following this rule. After all, investigative reporters James Bandler and Nicholas Varchaver remark, "Who would want to anger Madoff and risk losing their privileges?"[24]

Another reason that Madoff was able to fool so many investors so well and for so long was that he possessed an innate, highly effective ability to make people trust and believe in him. Sander sums it up this way:

> There in front of you [stands] a soft-spoken, gentle, kind, mild-mannered man with a boyish face, [and] a cute smile . . . a guy who would seem just as at home in his garden or in his study in a bathrobe as in an office. . . . You've known of his reputation for years. A super investor. [You] have enough money [to] invest with Bernie Madoff. Why not? What have you got to lose?[25]

As time went on, these personal qualities helped Madoff seal the deal with potential clients. Among the biggest was Carl Shapiro, who began giving him funds to invest in the 1960s. The wealthy clothing executive, who believed in Madoff right up until the end, was fated to lose some $545 million in the decades-long con.

A Fraudulent, Unstable System

Madoff frequently searched for new clients and asked Shapiro and other existing clients to invest more money. The reason that Madoff needed a steady stream of new funds and investors was that he was running what financial experts call a pyramid, or Ponzi, scheme. The term *Ponzi* comes from short-time bank manager and big-time swindler Charles Ponzi (1882–1949). An Italian immigrant, in 1920 he perpetrated a fraud that drew in some seventeen thousand investors. Each forked over to him money that they thought, based on his convincing claims, would quickly earn a handsome profit.

The problem was that Ponzi had no interest in managing or investing the money. His plan was to collect it and grow rich while pretending to be an honest money manager. As it turned out, he was not as smart, either as a businessman or criminal, as he thought, and the scheme collapsed in less than a year. (Ponzi was convicted and served several years in prison.) In fact, such schemes almost always collapse because they are inherently unstable and unpredictable. "The mechanics of a

Although Charles Ponzi, seen here, did not invent the scheme named for him, in 1920 he perpetrated a fraud on seventeen thousand investors.

Ponzi scheme are pretty simple," writes financial fraud expert Harry Markopolos.

> People are offered an opportunity to invest in a business that seems real and even logical . . . in return for unusually large and rapid profits. These initial investors get every dollar they were promised. They usually earn a profit large enough to make them boast about it to everyone they know. Other people rush to get into this business to receive the same kind of returns, sometimes begging the perpetrators to take their money. In fact, in a true Ponzi scheme there is no underlying business and there are no

The Swedish Match King

Charles Ponzi was not the only major swindler to perpetrate a huge financial fraud before Bernie Madoff came along. Perhaps the most famous of all was Sweden's Ivar Kreuger, who became known as the Swedish Match King. He bought up numerous match factories across Europe in the 1920s. Then he began loaning large sums of money to various European governments. France alone borrowed $75 million from him in 1927. Kreuger continued to buy new companies, but as time went on he was unable to make enough from his match business to cover what he spent. So he doctored his account books, reporting profits where none existed. Finally, the great 1929 stock market crash created a situation in which his scheme was exposed and quickly crumbled. His reputation ruined, in 1932 he shot himself to death.

Ivar Kreuger, the Swedish Match King, was a major financial swindler in the 1920s. His financial house of cards collapsed in the stock market crash of 1929, and he committed suicide three years later.

investments. There is nothing except the cash coming in and the cash going out. The initial investors are paid with seed money used to set up the scam. From that until the scheme collapses, investors are paid with funds received from later investors. Generally, a substantial number of these investors reinvest their supposed profits in the business. On paper, they can become wealthy, but only on paper. The scheme can last as long as new investors continue to hand over their money so old investors can be paid.[26]

Following this fraudulent, unstable system, Madoff collected investment funds from his clients but failed to actually invest any of the money. Instead, he paid some of the newer money to some of the older clients, claiming these were profits they had earned over time. Meanwhile, he kept large amounts of the money for himself. As long as he could keep drawing in new funds, and few clients asked to cash out all their monies, he could, in theory, keep the scam going.

To Madoff's relief, the scheme did keep rolling along, year after year, decade after decade. At some point in the 1980s, it surpassed $1 billion worth of investments. By 2000 that figure had reached about $7 billion, and by the end of 2005 it was nearing $50 billion. "What had started decades before as a small-time recruiting effort [at] country clubs had gone global," Bandler and Varchaver write. "Massive international institutions . . . were all funneling billions [to] Madoff, lured by the call of steady 10% to 12% returns."[27]

The problem for Madoff was that the bigger and more successful he got, the more attention he called to his illicit operation. Red flags were beginning to go up in a financial industry in which constantly high profits are considered too good to be true. Madoff himself began to worry that his financial empire was nearing the edge of a cliff, and he was right.

Chapter 4

Something Rotten in New York?

For at least four decades, Madoff benefited from his dual business, one side of which was legal and well-known, the other illegal and known to few. By the late 1970s, he was making millions of dollars a year, which allowed him and his wife, Ruth, to live quite well. From the small apartment in Bayside, Queens, where they lived right after their wedding, they moved to a moderate-sized ranch-style home in Roslyn, a small town on Long Island's northern shore. There, they began to raise two sons. Mark was born in 1964, and Andrew came along two years later. Both boys later joined their father's business—the legal stock-trading part—in the late 1980s after they had graduated college.

While growing up, Mark and Andrew never wanted for anything. Indeed, for as long as they could remember, their father had made more than a comfortable living. Madoff's financial success and consistent upward mobility can be conveniently traced through the homes that he and his wife purchased over the years. In 1981 they bought a large, $3 million house in the Hamptons, in eastern Long Island. Three years later the couple added to the Long Island house a roomy apartment on Manhattan's Upper East Side, just two blocks from scenic Central Park. It cost them a bit more than $3 million to buy at the time; today the same unit is estimated to be worth more than $7 million. Besides these dwellings, in 1994 the Madoffs purchased a five-bedroom, seven-bathroom waterfront mansion in Palm

Beach, Florida. It is estimated to be worth close to $10 million today. Also in Palm Beach, they had a 55-foot (17m) yacht named *Bull*. Finally, sometime in the 1990s the Madoffs bought a small villa in southern France. In addition to these personal residences, Madoff owned the extremely expensive space that housed his business. It consisted of three full floors of the well-known Lipstick Building on Manhattan's Third Avenue.

In addition to these costly personal assets, Madoff had a yearly income of millions of dollars. He also had positive notoriety on Wall Street, including multiple stints as chairman of the NASDAQ. To most people, he seemed to be the very model of a successful financial tycoon. The general wisdom was that he was a person who had started with nothing and through personal talent and hard work had achieved the American dream and much more.

The Model Citizen?

Yet a few select, savvy industry insiders were not so impressed with Madoff. When they thought about him and his still-growing financial empire, to paraphrase Shakespeare's *Hamlet*, they smelled something rotten in the state of New York (rather

A Desire for Solitude

Though he had an ability to make people feel comfortable around him, Madoff was not particularly comfortable around other people. Perhaps because he worried that outsiders might get too close to his secrets, according to his biographer Andrew Kirtzman, he was most content when alone in peaceful, quiet surroundings:

> Bernie was a quiet and distant man, never the sparkplug at a party or a dinner table. He didn't like meeting new people and could grow aloof [distant] among friends. He was happiest when he was alone, puttering on his 55-foot [yacht]. He seemed like someone endlessly in search of peace and quiet. He would often grow cranky and retreat to a corner in a room. "Stop yapping!" he'd yell when Ruth was on the phone or gossiping with a friend. . . . Friends sometimes worried about his desire for solitude. "Bernie always had a sense of worry about him," said one. When he seemed stressed, he would neither confide his problems nor explode over them. He would simply wander off, close his eyes, and take a nap.

Andrew Kirtzman, *Betrayal: The Life and Lies of Bernie Madoff*. New York: HarperCollins, 2009, pp. 59–61.

Bernie Madoff was happiest when he spent time secluded on his fifty-five-foot (17m) yacht, Bull.

than Denmark). In particular, they wondered how he could consistently make large profits for his investors even during those inevitable periodic times when the market was down. Among these doubters was Markopolos. He later said:

It was obvious, at least in my opinion, that the largest investment firms either knew or suspected that Madoff was a fraud. None of them—Merrill Lynch, Citigroup, Morgan Stanley— had invested with him. In fact, a managing director at

A "Level of Ingrained Dishonesty"

According to some observers, part of the reason that Madoff was able to live with the realization that he was stealing money from his own clients was that he had been hardened by the cutthroat, dog-eat-dog atmosphere of Wall Street, which seemed to have its own set of ethics. Harry Markopolos, who tried hard to get the Securities and Exchange Commission to investigate Madoff, describes that unnatural atmosphere this way:

What surprised me from the beginning of my career was the level of corruption that was simply an accepted way of doing business. Bernie Madoff wasn't a complete aberration [deviation from the norm]. He was an extension of the cutthroat culture that was prevalent from the day I started. This is not an indictment of the whole industry. The great majority of people I've met in this industry are honest and ethical. But in a business where money is the scoreboard, there is a certain level of ingrained dishonesty that is tolerated. I became disillusioned very quickly. I learned that the industry is based on predator-prey relationships. The equation is simple. If you don't know who the predator is, then you are the prey.

Harry Markopolos, *No One Would Listen*. New York: Wiley, 2010, p. 12.

Goldman Sachs's brokerage operation admitted to me that he didn't believe Madoff's returns were legitimate, so they had decided not to do business with him.[28]

These scattered, quiet, but nagging suspicions about Madoff by a handful of insiders simply would not go away. They resulted in a series of investigations of him and/or some of his financial associates in the 1990s and the decade that followed. The two most prominent of those associates were Bienes and Avellino, the accountants who had long worked for Alpern, Madoff's father-in-law. Over the years, Bienes and Avellino had made millions of dollars referring their clients to Madoff's supposedly real money management operation. (Madoff paid a hefty kickback to the accountants for each of their clients who ended up investing money with him.)

In 1992 someone in the SEC got wind that Bienes and Avellino were not licensed to take people's money for the purpose of investing it. It came out that the two accountants had long been luring in potential investors and promising them returns, or profits, of 13.5 to 20 percent. Worried that Bienes and Avellino might be running some sort of pyramid scheme or other major swindle, SEC officials got a court injunction to temporarily close their business.

During the investigation that followed, the officials learned that the accountants had not been trying to invest the money themselves; rather, they had been handing the clients over to Madoff, presumably to be processed through his legitimate brokerage arm. Because Bienes and Avellino had broken the law by doing this without a license, any and all funds that they had channeled toward Madoff were now seen as tainted.

At this point, however, Madoff stepped in and offered to return all the money the accountants had originally raised for him from clients—amounting to $441 million in all. The SEC officials apparently viewed this as an honest, generous gesture by Madoff. Considering his excellent reputation on Wall Street, the SEC did not bother to investigate him at all. Indeed, it never even took criminal action against the accountants. The two men agreed to pay a combined civil fine of $350,000 and walked away largely unscathed.

Years later, a number of observers noted how Madoff had managed to dodge the bullet, so to speak, in the 1992 investigation. Once more he had used the first-rate reputation of the legitimate arm of his business, along with his charm and smooth talking, to avert suspicion from his massive ongoing fraud. According to two *Fortune* magazine investigators:

> What's striking is that Madoff appears to have played the role of model citizen in this case. Billing records show that [the SEC officials] held multiple phone conversations and at least one meeting with Madoff, who was able to provide investing records when Avellino & Bienes couldn't. They also show Madoff personally handling requests for computer records and the like, the sort of routine queries that in almost any other firm would have been handed off to the chief technology officer or a more junior person. Madoff's personal touch seemed to score points. [One official] testified that Madoff was "forthright" in answering his questions.[29]

A "Void of Indifference"

Madoff became the focus of scrutiny a second time in 1999. This time the probe was not instigated by the SEC but rather by two financial trade magazines—*Mar/Hedge* and *Barron's*. The editors of these publications had learned, behind the scenes, that Madoff was managing money for an unknown number of investors. Each magazine ran an article that asked questions about that operation, which the grapevine claimed involved client funds worth at least $6 billion to $7 billion. If true, the articles said, Madoff's investment business constituted the largest or second-largest hedge fund in the world. (A hedge fund is a legitimate investment account that is open to a limited number of large investors and attempts to grow their initial money by placing it with a wide range of companies and types of investments.) The articles also questioned Madoff's ability to earn consistent profits of 15 percent or more for his clients, month after month, year after year. Such steady, uninterrupted success was for the most part unheard of in the investment markets, they pointed out.

As in the 1992 SEC investigation, Madoff personally answered the questions the magazines had raised. First, pouring on the charm, he acted as if the inquiry was so off base that he found it amusing. As for his ability to earn consistent profits for his customers, he said, it was nothing more than some old-fashioned good luck. The market had been doing well overall in recent times, and he had taken advantage of it. Any suggestions that something illegitimate was going on were simply ridiculous, he added.

The reporters who wrote the articles did not completely accept Madoff's explanation. But neither did they out-and-out accuse him of lying or evasion. As a result, the articles just came and went, in the process making no more than a tiny ripple in the enormous, wildly turbulent Wall Street pond. In the later words of the *Fortune* magazine investigators: "What seemed like clear warnings disappeared into a void of indifference."[30]

The Math Did Not Add Up

The next, and potentially most damaging, probe into Madoff's financial dealings came in 2005 and 2006. This SEC investigation was prompted in part by the urgings of Markopolos. He had been telling SEC officials for years that he suspected Madoff was a con artist running a criminal enterprise. In 2000 the heads of the Boston-based Rampart Investment Management Company had asked Markopolos to do some serious research and figure out Madoff's investment strategy. They could then try to replicate it and reap the benefits. But the more Markopolos examined the case, the more the math did not add up, so to speak. He finally concluded that Madoff was in reality defrauding people, very likely using a classic Ponzi scheme.

In 2005 Markopolos, who saw it as his patriotic duty to expose Madoff and prevent his victims from suffering irreversible losses, sent a twenty-one-page memo to SEC regulators. It outlined in detail the many red flags he had unearthed regarding Madoff's fraud. But the officials ended up doing very little. They did briefly examine Madoff, questioning whether he was properly registered to act as an investment adviser for a set number of clients. According to the rules, any money manager with fifteen

Financial expert and part-time investigator Harry Markopolos's accusations to the SEC that Madoff was a fraud and a con artist prompted the commission's investigation.

or more large-scale investor-clients had to be specially registered.

Yet again, Madoff managed to run the obstacle course of official questions. Interviewed by the SEC in May 2006, he lied, claiming that he had very few clients whose money he managed. Furthermore, he said, several of his clients were based in Europe, outside the jurisdiction of the SEC, which regulated only U.S. markets. The regulators did tell Madoff that to be technically in compliance with the rules, he needed to register properly. When he immediately and dutifully offered to do so, they closed the case in November 2006, saying in part:

> The staff found no evidence of fraud. The staff did find, however, that BLM [Bernard L. Madoff] acted as an investment advisor in certain hedge funds . . . in violation of the registration requirements of the Advisors Act. . . . As a result of discussions with the staff, BLM registered . . . [so] we recommend closing this investigation because [BLM] voluntarily remedied the uncovered violations, and because those violations were not so serious as to warrant enforcement actions.[31]

In this way, Madoff yet again escaped close scrutiny of his giant investment scam. At the same time, the SEC had once more failed to uncover the fraud, a misstep that would later

Duties of the SEC

Numerous observers of the Madoff affair have commented that the Securities and Exchange Commission (SEC), the organization tasked with regulating Wall Street, failed to uncover his scam and thereby to protect the public. The following description of the SEC's purpose and responsibilities comes from its official Web site.

> The mission of the U.S. Securities and Exchange Commission is to protect investors, maintain fair, orderly, and efficient markets, and facilitate capital formation. . . . The laws and rules that govern the securities industry in the United States derive from a simple and straightforward concept: all investors, whether large institutions or private individuals, should have access to certain basic facts about an investment prior to buying it, and so long as they hold it. To achieve this, the SEC requires public companies to disclose meaningful financial and other information to the public. . . . Only through the steady flow of timely, comprehensive, and accurate information can people make sound investment decisions. . . . It is the responsibility of the Commission to: interpret federal securities laws; issue new rules and amend existing rules; oversee the inspection of securities firms, brokers, investment advisers, and ratings agencies; oversee private regulatory organizations in the securities, accounting, and auditing fields; and coordinate U.S. securities regulation with federal, state, and foreign authorities.

MADOFF
Stole it

SEC
Ignored it

SEC, "The Investor's Advocate: How the SEC Protects Investors, Maintains Market Integrity, and Facilitates Capital Formation." www.sec.gov/about/whatwedo .shtml.

Numerous observers think the Securities and Exchange Commission failed to uncover Madoff's scam and protect the public.

make it look clumsy, if not incompetent. As Sander says, the SEC's 2006 oversight was "kind of like issuing a ticket for an expired driver's license—and nothing more—to a driver responsible for crashing into a bus and killing thirty people."[32]

At this point Markopolos, for one, began to worry that Madoff might be too hard to bring down. In some ways, it looked as if he was so well entrenched and crafty that he might be untouchable.

The round-shaped building in the foreground housed the Bernard L. Madoff Investment Securities firm. In 2006 Madoff was able to lie his way out of another SEC investigation.

Did Madoff Suffer From OCD?

Some investigators and writers who have closely studied the Madoff case have concluded that Bernie Madoff is at least marginally obsessive-compulsive. Obsessive-compulsive disorder (OCD) is a condition in which a person engages in a series of repetitive behaviors or pays abnormal attention to detail in order to reduce or relieve deep-seated anxieties. Possibly Madoff was so haunted by his dishonesty and worried that his financial schemes would be exposed that he displayed various examples of obsessive-compulsive behavior. Those who knew him well reported that he would often go from room to room in his office suite and make sure that the blinds were all drawn to the same level. He also insisted that all computer screens in a room stand at the same height and that all of his employees use black ink pens.

But as it turned out, this worry was misplaced. Although the wily Madoff had been able to slip through the clutches of numerous individuals and organizations, he had yet to face an adversary he had no chance of beating. This was the sometimes volatile and always unpredictable market itself. It was about to take a major unexpected turn, one that would bring Wall Street's greatest crook to his knees.

Chapter 5

His Scheme Exposed at Last

A t almost 8:30 A.M. on December 11, 2008, two FBI agents, Ted Cacioppi and B.J. King, walked up to the door of Madoff's Manhattan penthouse apartment on Sixty-fourth Street and knocked. A few seconds later, Madoff, still dressed in his pajamas, slippers, and bathrobe, appeared and let them in. After a brief question-and-answer session, the agents told him to get dressed. Then they handcuffed him and took him to FBI head-quarters at New York City's Federal Plaza. There, he was allowed to phone his lawyer, Ira Lee Sorkin. "Ike," Madoff said, "it's Bernie. I'm in the FBI office and I'm handcuffed to a chair."[33] Sorkin responded, "Bernie, don't say another thing."[34]

But it was too late. Madoff had already briefly described his financial fraud to Cacioppi and King. His secret was finally out. Looking back on his rise and fall, various observers have pointed out that indeed, secrecy had always been the key to his success. As long as no one knew what he was really doing to the unsuspecting victims of his large-scale investment swindle, he could sustain that fraud and the lavish lifestyle it had helped to finance. But once the cloak of secrecy had been removed, he was revealed for what he truly was—a career criminal who had never been as talented, wise, and refined as most people had as-sumed. In truth, it had all been, in the words of a familiar adage, mostly smoke and mirrors. As his nemesis Markopolos later put it, Madoff "was simply a guy you gave your money to, to do whatever he wanted to do with it, and in return he handed you

DAILY◉NEWS

75¢   **2.5 MILLION READERS EVERY DAY**   NYDailyNews.com

FREE! FINANCIAL ADVICE FOR EVERY READER
COMING MONDAY — SEE PAGES 22-23

DISROBED!

- **FBI busted Bernie in his bathrobe**
- **Mets' owners lost millions in 50B scam**

Bernie Madoff told agents: "There is no innocent explanation."

PAGES 6-7

YANKS SIGN A.J. TO JOIN CC SEE SPORTS

The December 13, 2008, edition of the New York Daily News made fun of Madoff's bathrobed attire during his arrest by FBI agents.

a nice profit. He was the Wizard of Oz, and he made everybody so happy that they didn't want to look behind the curtain [and see things as they really were]."[35]

The Beginning of the End

Why would Madoff so suddenly and purposely reveal his well-guarded secret and turn himself in to the authorities? The simple answer, according to the many investigators, writers, and others who later studied the case, was that he felt he had no other choice. Forces beyond his control had put him in a position in which no matter how secretive or careful or charming he was or acted, his complex monetary scheme could no longer support itself. The framework of his financial empire was abruptly collapsing around him, and he could do nothing else but try to keep himself from being completely buried in the rubble.

The causes of that financial collapse had not targeted Madoff —nor any other individual or company. Rather, they were market- and system-driven trends and events, pushed and pulled by dozens of unfeeling, unknowing financial, social, and political forces that had been building for some time.

Among the more powerful of these forces was the decline of the U.S. housing market. Beginning in 2007, it rapidly lost trillions of dollars of value, and millions of people could no longer afford to pay their mortgages. Banks and other big financial institutions held these mortgages, so they lost money, too. The result was that, as the housing market crashed, most banks slowed their rate of lending, so much so that large numbers of people of all walks of life could no longer obtain loans. Like a gigantic game of musical chairs, these events caused a ripple effect throughout the country's economy, making money increasingly tight and investors more nervous and cautious.

Madoff now faced a cold, hard fact. Namely, a downward-spiraling national economy automatically sounds the death knell of large Ponzi schemes. The reason is simple and straightforward, as exemplified by Madoff's case. For years most of those who had given him their money, convinced that he was investing it, had been content to leave it alone and allow it to grow. But now,

Other Recent Ponzi Schemers

When Madoff's fraud went public, many people were surprised that he had managed to operate a large Ponzi scheme for so long. But the reality was that he was not the only person in recent times who had tried to bilk people using that method. In 1985, for example, a San Diego financial trader named David Dominelli swindled more than one thousand investors out of a total of $80 million before he was caught. Even more successful was self-styled religious leader Gerald Payne, who claimed that God had given him tips on the most lucrative investments. Payne got upward of twenty thousand people to give him money—about $500 million in all—that they thought he was investing in precious metals

like gold. In 2003 Reed Slatkin, who cofounded the online service Earth-Link, was sentenced to fourteen years in prison. His crime was to operate a Ponzi scheme that cheated investors out of a total of $250 million.

EarthLink cofounder Reed Slatkin received a fourteen-year federal prison sentence for a Ponzi scheme that bilked his investors of $250 million.

with so much financial uncertainty in the real estate and other markets, fear became the operative word. Many of Madoff's clients decided to withdraw their money from him so that they could pay off other debts or use the money in other ways.

These attempts to cash in the funds Madoff had supposedly been investing spelled almost instant disaster for him. The requests totaled more than $7 billion, which the clients assumed Madoff had easy access to. But in reality he did not. Because he had been running a Ponzi scheme, the money had never been invested and had long ago been paid out or spent. The only way Madoff could hope to get his hands on such large-scale funds was to find new investors, whose fresh money would hopefully keep the enormous scam afloat long enough to avert catastrophe. In desperation, Madoff turned to his old friend Shapiro and asked him to invest more cash. Shapiro, who still thought he was working with an honest, fabulously talented money manager, came through and handed over $250,000. Madoff promised to pay it all back, both swiftly and with interest.

Meanwhile, Madoff began to buckle under the increasing stress and strain. He started having adverse physical and mental reactions to what appeared to be his impending ruin. His long-faithful secretary, Eleanor Squillari, became aware that his blood pressure was erratic and often too high. "He was taking blood pressure medicine and his back was killing him," she later told investigators. "He was walking crooked and we tried to give him a pain patch. He could make it through meetings with investors, but then he would collapse afterward. I'd see him lying on the floor. His eyes would be closed and his arms outstretched, like a dead person."[36]

"I'm Finished"

Finally, Madoff could take no more. Many years before, he had recognized that the odds of his large-scale scam being uncovered would increase over time, and sooner or later he might well be caught and punished. Now, he reasoned regrettably, that awful day of reckoning was upon him. On December 10, 2008, he met with his sons, Mark and Andrew, at his Manhattan apartment. According to their recollections, he admitted to them that he was a world-class phony. "It's all just one big lie," he said, "basically a giant Ponzi scheme." He told them how for years he had defrauded his so-called investors. "I'm finished!" he blurted out. "I have absolutely nothing."[37]

Bernie Madoff's Ponzi scheme was brought down by a combination of financial factors, not the least of which was the collapse of the housing market in 2007.

Having spilled his guts to his sons, Madoff asked them to keep quiet for a week or so while he got his affairs in order, after which they should turn him in to the authorities. It is uncertain what he meant by "affairs." One might assume he was referring to his will and family relationships. However, evidence later surfaced indicating that he planned to divide up the $250,000 Shapiro had recently given him and pay it out as bonuses to key family members and employees.

As it turned out, however, time would not allow any more of Madoff's schemes to unfold. Immediately after leaving the meeting with their father, Mark and Andrew Madoff hired a lawyer named Martin Flumenbaum. He advised them to talk to the FBI and SEC right away. If they waited a week, as their father had asked them to, he warned, it would look like they were conspiring with him in his crimes. The young men prudently took this advice and quickly informed the appropriate authorities.

Their tip-off to the FBI triggered the visit by agents Cacioppi and King to Bernie Madoff's apartment the next morning. "Do you know why we're here?" Cacioppi asked. He then answered his own question, saying that he and King had come "to find out if there is an innocent explanation" for the allegations Madoff's sons had made the night before. After a tense pause, Madoff answered, "There is no innocent explanation."[38] He went on to tell the agents that everything Mark and Andrew had said was true. The investment business he had been operating for years was crooked and a big Ponzi scheme. Cacioppi then waited for Madoff to get dressed, read him his rights, and led him away.

Preliminary Court Rulings

On his way to FBI headquarters, Madoff mulled over what was about to happen to him. He knew that he would be charged with running a Ponzi scheme and stealing millions of dollars' worth of his clients' funds. However, whether he realized he was also guilty of and would be charged with the crime of affinity fraud is unclear. According to Markopolos, an affinity scheme targets people with similar affiliations. Bernie was Jewish, so he targeted the New York metropolitan area [where a lot of Jews lived] and Florida Jewish communities. Historically, almost by definition, Ponzi schemes start within a well-defined community, often an ethnic or religious community. If I were trying to start a Ponzi scheme, for example, I would do it inside the Greek community [because Markopolos is Greek]. The reason for that is trust. Nobody thinks one of their own is going to cheat them.[39]

Eventually, a judge would give due weight to the affinity fraud and the breach of trust it entailed when sentencing Madoff. For the moment, however, the first matter to come before a judge in the Madoff case concerned the amount of Madoff's bail. On the day of the arrest, December 11, bail was set at $10 million. (The bail was secured, or guaranteed, by Madoff's Manhattan apartment and some of his other properties. If he had chosen to skip bail and run away, the state would have confiscated these expensive properties.)

At first, the judge said that Madoff could travel around southern New York and Connecticut, where most of his business dealings took place. But this was soon changed to house arrest because the prosecutors worried that the accused man might try to escape the country. Thereafter, Madoff had to remain in the Manhattan apartment except when called to appear in court.

Still another preliminary court ruling froze Madoff's assets, or disallowed him from accessing and using his bank accounts, homes, boats, and other properties. These assets were worth many millions of dollars. The judge wanted to make sure that he did not dispose of them in some sneaky way before the court was able to divide them among his victims.

Those victims began to hear about Madoff's scam almost immediately after his arrest. One of them, Bette Greenfield, in her seventies, read the ugly truth in the *Wall Street Journal* the day after the FBI took Madoff into custody. Her father had invested his life savings with Madoff in the 1990s. When the father died, it had amounted to $400,000, which Bette and her two brothers

After his arrest, Madoff was able to post a $10 million bond that allowed him to roam around his Manhattan neighborhood. Prosecutors, fearing Madoff would leave the country, later had the courts place him under house arrest in his Manhattan apartment.

had come to count on for their retirement. Horrified to discover that the money might be gone forever, she remarked, "I really was like in shock, non-believing shock. This couldn't have happened. This didn't happen. This is—oh my God, what am I going to do?"[40] Words similar to these were repeated by Madoff's many other victims in the weeks and months that followed. Along with millions of shocked people around the world, they closely watched a New York court gear up to mete out some long overdue justice to Bernie Madoff.

Chapter 6

Madoff Guilty on All Charges

After Madoff's sons turned him in to the authorities in December 2008, the legal system in New York State began to process his case. Because he had admitted his guilt and did not intend to contest that he had broken the law, no formal trial was scheduled. Instead, a plea hearing was planned for March 2009. In it, Madoff would face a judge, admit to breaking the law, describe his crimes in considerable detail, and listen as the judge listed the charges against him and explained the maximum penalties that might be meted out for each charge. At the end of the hearing, a date would be set for a second court appearance in which Madoff would be sentenced to whatever punishments the court deemed appropriate.

In the meantime, Madoff awaited his fate in his posh Manhattan apartment. He had easily met the $10 million bail requirement set in December and was allowed to avoid jail as long as he remained in the apartment. But this was not good enough for the prosecutors of Madoff's case. One of them, U.S. attorney Marc O. Litt, argued that Madoff's bail should be revoked and that he should await his hearings in jail. First, Litt said, Madoff had mailed packages containing various valuables to his sons, brother, and some friends in late December. This was a clear violation of his bail agreement. Second, Litt insisted, if Madoff was not imprisoned, he might try to flee. Litt stated: "The case against the defendant is strong and it continues to grow stronger as the government's investigation continues.

Madoff's attorney Ira Sorkin was able to keep his client out of jail before his plea allocution.

Given the defendant's age, the length of the likely sentence, [and] the strength of the proof against the defendant, including his confessions, these facts present a clear risk of flight."[41] Sorkin countered that his client was not a flight risk and, at least for the moment, managed to keep Madoff out of jail.

Who Else Was Involved?

While Madoff was awaiting his plea hearing, New York prosecutors vigorously continued to uncover facts about his crimes. In particular, they sought to find out if he had acted alone. As one expert observer puts it, they had ample reason to suspect that others had been involved in what was emerging as the largest known financial swindle in history:

> It would have been too big for one person, especially when one considers the administrative tasks. Tallying month-end figures, preparing statements, [filling out] tax statements, [performing] SEC filings—how did all of that get done, and who actually performed the tasks? . . . There must have been a team buying and selling stocks, forging books, and filing reports.[42]

Of the possible coconspirators in the Madoff case, prosecutors considered several possible suspects. They included, among others, Madoff's wife, Ruth; his sons, Mark and Andrew; his brother, Peter; David Friehling, an outside accountant who worked for Madoff over several years; and Frank DiPascali, who began working for Madoff in 1975 and became chief financial officer (CFO) of the company in 1996.

The prosecutors suspected that Madoff had kept his closest family members in the dark about his illegal schemes, probably to protect them if and when said schemes were found out. Indeed, the general consensus that emerged about Ruth Madoff was that, as *New York Times* reporters David Segal and Alison L. Cowan suggest, "One day, she was married to a stock-market genius, the next she was married to one of history's great con men."[43]

In contrast, prosecutors reasoned that Madoff was likely to be less sentimental about involving nonfamily members in his

Rip-Offs Right up to the End

The prosecutors who brought Bernie Madoff to trial frequently portrayed him as a dishonest, unfeeling crook who had no compassion for his fellow human beings and felt no remorse for bilking thousands of people out of their life savings. Part of the proof of this accusation was the discovery that on December 3, just eight days before Madoff gave himself up to FBI agents, he completed still another blatant rip-off of an unsuspecting investor. Martin Rosenman, of Great Neck, New York, the boss of a heating-oil company, had been referred to Madoff by a friend. Rosenman said that he wanted to invest $10 million, and Madoff agreed. The deal went through on December 9, two days before the great Ponzi scheme collapsed. Rosenman's sad loss demonstrated that right up to the end, Madoff had no hesitation about ruining other peoples' lives.

scam. Accordingly, Friehling and DiPascali both came under increasing scrutiny by government investigators in 2009. In particular, investigators felt it was hard to believe that Madoff's CFO could have discharged his duties efficiently year after year if he had known nothing about the ongoing fraud.

The Plea Allocution

Before investigators could finish building their case against DiPascali, however, it was time for Madoff's own first court hearing. On March 12, 2009, accompanied by his attorney, Madoff stood before Judge Denny Chin in a New York district court. Following standard procedure for a plea hearing, Chin asked the defendant if he understood that he had a right to a full trial. No one was forcing him to plead guilty, Chin pointed out. Moreover, if Madoff so desired, he could plead not guilty,

be represented by an attorney, and proceed to bring his case before a jury. Chin added: "Do you understand that by pleading guilty today you are giving up each and every one of these rights, you are waving these rights, and you will have no trial?" On Sorkin's advice (in strategy sessions held before the hearing), Madoff quietly answered, "I do."[44]

Once these formalities were out of the way, Chin read the charges against Madoff. Eleven in all, they included fraud, theft, money laundering, perjury, wire fraud, theft from an employee

In this courtroom rendering, Bernie Madoff pleads guilty to a $50 billion Ponzi scheme in a Manhattan federal court. He was immediately placed in handcuffs and taken to jail.

benefit plan, and making false filings to the SEC. The judge also stated the legal penalty for each charge.

Next, Madoff presented his plea allocution. It consisted of a prepared speech in which he admitted his wrongdoing and explained how it had occurred. Carefully drafted with Sorkin's aid and advice, the speech gave Madoff a chance to try to make the best impression he could on the judge and court by being straightforward and apologetic about his crimes. This tone of honesty and humility is fully apparent in the opening section, in which he briefly identified his misdeeds and apologized for them:

A Strategy Never Used

In this excerpt from his plea allocution, delivered to the court in March 2009, Madoff explains his so-called split strike conversion strategy. As he readily admits, he never actually used this method, which he told his clients he was using to invest their money.

> While I never promised a specific rate of return to any client, I felt compelled to satisfy my clients' expectations, at any cost. I therefore claimed that I employed an investment strategy I had developed, called a "split strike conversion strategy," to falsely give the appearance to clients that I had achieved the results I believed they expected. Through the split-strike conversion strategy, I promised to clients and prospective clients that client funds would be invested in a basket of common stocks within the Standard & Poor's 100 Index, a collection of the 100 largest publicly traded companies in terms of their market capitalization. I promised that I would select a basket of stocks that would closely mimic the price movements of the Standard & Poor's 100 Index. I promised that I would opportunistically time these purchases and would be out of the market intermittently, investing client funds during these periods in United States Government-issued securities such as United States Treasury bills. . . . In fact, I never made the investments I promised clients, who believed they were invested with me in the split strike conversion strategy.

Your Honor, for many years up until my arrest on December 11, 2008, I operated a Ponzi scheme through the investment advisory side of my business, Bernard L. Madoff Securities LLC. . . . I am actually grateful for this first opportunity to publicly speak about my crimes, for which I am so deeply sorry and ashamed. . . . I am painfully aware that I have deeply hurt many, many people, including the members of my family, my closest friends, business associates, and the thousands of clients who gave me their money. I cannot adequately express how sorry I am for what I have done. I am here today to accept responsibility for my crimes by pleading guilty and, with this plea allocution, explain the means by which I carried out and concealed my fraud.[45]

Then Madoff described the exact nature of the financial fraud he had perpetrated:

The essence of my scheme was that I represented to clients and prospective clients . . . that I would invest their money in shares of common stock, options, and other securities of well-known corporations, and upon request, would return to them their profits and principle. Those representations were false because for many years and up until I was arrested on December 11, 2008, I never invested those funds in securities, as I had promised. Instead, those funds were deposited in a bank account at Chase Manhattan Bank. When clients wished to receive the profits they believed they had earned with me or to redeem their principal, I used the money in the Chase Manhattan bank account that belonged to them or other clients to pay the requested funds. The victims of my scheme included individuals, charitable organizations, trusts, pension funds and hedge funds.[46]

A Plea for Leniency

Chin listened patiently as Madoff slowly and at times quite obviously painfully described how he had orchestrated and covered up his illegal financial scam. When the defendant's speech had

Madoff stands before Judge Chin during his sentencing hearing on June 29, 2009.

concluded, the judge, again following standard procedure, asked Madoff whether he was guilty or not guilty of the crimes he had just described to the court. Madoff meekly said guilty, soon after which Chin set a sentencing date for the following June (2009).

Sorkin then spoke up, boldly addressing the topic of his client's bail. Madoff was not a flight risk, Sorkin claimed, and therefore should be allowed to remain free on bail until the sentencing hearing. However, Chin disagreed, saying:

As Mr. Madoff has pled guilty, he is no longer entitled to the presumption of innocence [as he had been before his plea]. In light of Mr. Madoff's age, he has an incentive to flee, he has the means to flee, and thus, he presents a risk of flight. Bail is revoked, and the defendant is remanded [held in custody].[47]

Having pled guilty, Madoff began preparing for the sentencing hearing scheduled for June. Perhaps not surprisingly, he and Sorkin began focusing their energies on convincing the judge to grant leniency. They drafted a letter to the court, stating

A Betrayal of Trust

In addition to stealing money in a huge Ponzi scheme, Madoff lured many of his victims into an affinity fraud, in which members of a particular ethnic or religious group are targeted. Lisa Fairfax, a professor of law at George Washington University Law School, explains why such a betrayal of trust works so well:

> Relying on group trust is often so powerful in overcoming people's skepticism that both the financially unsophisticated and the seemingly sophisticated fall victim to the scam. . . . Most investors [are] just looking for someone to trust so that they don't have to worry or otherwise pay attention. By relying on the trust common to many groups, affinity fraud makes people feel like they have found that someone. [Also] it is not at all unusual for affinity fraud scams to last significantly longer than other frauds. This is because once the trust is established, not only are investors less likely to fully investigate the scam, but they also are less likely to believe they have been defrauded, and even when they do believe, less likely to report outside of the group.

Lisa Fairfax, "Madoff and Affinity Fraud," *Concurring Opinions*. www.concurringopinions.com/archives/2010/03/madoff-and-affinity-fraud.html.

that Madoff was not looking for sympathy or mercy. Rather, he wanted only justice. The letter points out that several written statements had recently been filed in court by Madoff's victims, all of whom were naturally angry and wanted to see him suffer. Responding to that hostility, the leniency letter says in part:

> We believe that the unified tone of the victims' statements supports a desire for a type of mob vengeance that . . . would negate and render meaningless the role of the Court. Instead, we respectfully submit that it is the duty of the Court to set aside the emotion and hysteria attendant to this case and render a sentence that is just and proportionate to the conduct at issue. . . . Mr. Madoff [has] accepted full responsibility for his actions and expressed regret and remorse for those victimized by his scheme. . . . Furthermore, Mr. Madoff indicated at a very early stage his desire to cooperate. [Also] in light of the non-violent nature of his offense, Mr. Madoff should be sentenced to a term of years short of effective life imprisonment. Mr. Madoff is currently 71 years old and has an approximate life expectancy of 13 years. A prison term of 12 years . . . would sufficiently address goals of deterrence, protecting the public, and promoting respect for the law.[48]

The question, of course, was whether Judge Chin would be moved by these words. Would he show leniency, as Madoff and Sorkin hoped? Or would he satisfy the rage expressed by the victims of the scam and give the defendant a stiff penalty? More certain was that Madoff's case had attracted widespread attention in the media, and on June 29, 2009, when he faced the judge once more, the whole world would be watching.

Chapter 7

A Monster Faces His Victims

One after another, Madoff's victims stood up and condemned him. Some faced him, while others could not bear to look at him. But all echoed similar words and themes, calling him a thief and a monster. All felt they were in a sense kindred spirits with one of their number, Sharon Lissauer, who expressed her emotional devastation this way: "He killed my spirit and shattered my dreams. He destroyed my trust in people. He destroyed my life."[49]

The moving, often heart-rending scene took place in a spacious chamber in a New York district court on June 29, 2009. There, along with the victims and their supporters, legions of press people and other interested observers crowded around. Some pointed and sneered at Madoff, who sat silent at the defendant's desk with his attorney. For both the victims and press people, it was a banner day. After months of waiting anxiously, they would finally bear witness to the wheels of justice catching up to Madoff. Judge Chin, the same official who had accepted Madoff's guilty plea the preceding March, was scheduled to pass sentence on the perpetrator of the biggest, most heinous financial swindle in the country's history. Many of those in attendance, both inside and outside the courtroom—victims and ordinary concerned citizens alike—were tense and fretful. They were ready to express their outrage if Madoff, by this time viewed as a sort of supervillain in American society, did not receive a punishment that matched the severity of his crimes.

The Beast Must Be Caged

Chin began the proceedings by hearing from victims of Madoff's scam. Of the 113 victims' statements entered into the record, most took the form of letters, while some of those who had contributed written statements also showed up to speak their minds in person. One statement came from Randy Baird, who explained that she and her husband had put in

> a total of 67 years of hard work [with our] money saved and invested in [Madoff's company]. Our savings, our IRAs, 401Ks, our pension monies, all entrusted to [Madoff], and all gone. We are too old to make up what we lost. We have to start over. It's too painful to look back. [Madoff] robbed us not only of our money, but of our faith in humanity and in the systems in place that were supposed to protect us. Please remember his victims. Sentence this monster named Madoff to the most severe punishment within your abilities. . . . Please do the right thing and hold him accountable for his crimes.[50]

Madoff victim Sheryl Weinstein expressed the sentiments of many of Madoff's victims when she told the judge that Madoff was a beast who should be caged.

Other victims' statements sounded hauntingly similar to Baird's. Each pointed out that Madoff had done more than merely steal money; he had also made those who had trusted him feel like they could no longer trust anyone. For example, another victim of the massive Ponzi scheme, Jesse L. Cohen, told the judge:

> Madoff is a thief and a monster. He has stolen more than money. He has severely damaged my life and my elderly parents' lives. My parents, who were also Madoff investors, have lost their life savings for three generations. [They] are devastated, forced to live only on social security payments. . . . He ruined lives. He deserves no mercy. . . . Please make sure that the [prison] facility in which he is housed is extremely uncomfortable.[51]

Still another victim, Sheryl Weinstein, denounced Madoff as "a beast" who walks and blends in among the populace. "Your Honor," she told Judge Chin, "put this beast in the cage where it belongs."[52]

The Defense and Prosecution Speak

After the victims' statements had been made, the judge turned to Sorkin, the head of the defense team, who made a final plea for leniency. "We represent a deeply flawed individual," he admitted. Yet Madoff was also a human being with rights and needs of his own, Sorkin pointed out. "The magnificence of our legal system," the attorney continued, "is that we do not seek an eye for an eye." Similarly, "vengeance is not the goal of punishment. Our system of justice . . . has recognized that justice is and must be blind and fair. . . . Mr. Madoff is 71 years old, your Honor. Based upon his health . . . his family history, [and] his life expectancy, that is why we ask for a sentence of twelve years."[53]

Chin thanked Sorkin for his remarks and asked the defendant if he wanted to say anything in his own behalf. Madoff nodded and made a brief speech that said in part:

> Your Honor, I cannot offer you an excuse for my behavior. How do you excuse betraying thousands of investors who

entrusted me with their life savings? How do you excuse deceiving 200 employees who have spent most of their working life working for me? How do you excuse lying to your brother and two sons who spent their whole adult life helping to build a successful and respectful business? How do you excuse lying and deceiving a wife who stood by you for 50 years, and still stands by you? And how do you excuse deceiving an industry that you spent a better part of your life trying to improve? There is no excuse for that, and I don't ask any forgiveness. Although I may not have intended any harm, I did a great deal of harm. . . . I live in a tormented state now knowing of all the pain and suffering that I have created. I have left a legacy of shame, as some of my victims have pointed out, to my family and my grandchildren. That's something I will live with for the rest of my life. . . . I apologize to my victims. I will turn and face you. I am sorry. I know that doesn't help you. Your Honor, thank you for listening to me.[54]

Any sympathy that Madoff's speech may have created in the courtroom was instantly countered and erased by the remarks made by the prosecution. As Assistant U.S. Attorney Lisa A. Baroni spoke on behalf of herself, her colleagues on the prosecution team, and the people of New York State, her voice was filled with contempt. "This defendant carried out a fraud of unprecedented proportion over the course of more than a generation," she began.

For more than twenty years he stole ruthlessly and without remorse. Thousands of people placed their trust in him and he lied repeatedly to all of them. And as the Court heard from all of the victims, in their words and in the letters, he destroyed a lifetime of hard work of thousands of victims. And he used that victims' money to enrich himself and his family, with an opulent [lavish] lifestyle, homes around the world, yachts, private jets, and tens of millions of dollars of loans to his family. . . . The government respectfully requests that the court sentence the defendant to 150 years in prison or a substantial term of imprisonment that ensures that he will spend the rest of his life in jail.[55]

Ruth Madoff Speaks Her Mind

Shortly after her husband was sentenced to prison for his financial crimes, Ruth Madoff told the media:

> I am breaking my silence now, because my reluctance to speak has been interpreted as indifference or lack of sympathy for the victims of my husband Bernie's crime, which is exactly the opposite of the truth. From the moment I learned from my husband that he had committed an enormous fraud, I have had two thoughts—first, that so many people who trusted him would be ruined financially and emotionally, and second, that my life with the man I have known for over 50 years was over. Many of my husband's investors were my close friends and family. And in the days since December, I have read, with immense pain, the wrenching stories of people whose life savings have evaporated because of his crime. . . . In the end, to say that I feel devastated for the many whom my husband has destroyed is truly inadequate. Nothing I can say seems sufficient regarding the daily suffering that all those innocent people are enduring because of my husband.

Quoted in *Wall Street Journal*, "Ruth Madoff Issues Statement Regarding Husband's Fraud," June 29, 2009. http://online.wsj.com/article/SB124629343582068785.html.

Ruth Madoff was devastated by the enormity of her husband's crimes—many of her friends and family lost their life savings.

Not Just a Matter of Money

Finally, it was time for the judge to deliver the eagerly awaited sentence, a handful of words that would decide Madoff's fate for the rest of his days. It quickly became clear that Chin had been swayed much more by the sentiments of the prosecution and victims than by the defense and Madoff himself. Chin's tone was professional and businesslike. Yet in his voice was a hint of sternness and rebuke that clearly gave solace to the many victims who were listening. He started by addressing the issue of mob mentality, which Sorkin had brought up earlier:

> Despite all the emotion in the air, I do not agree with the suggestion that the victims and others are seeking mob vengeance. The fact that many have sounded similar themes does not mean that they are acting together as a mob. I do agree that a just and proportionate sentence must be determined, objectively, and without hysteria or undue emotion. Objectively speaking, the fraud here was staggering. It spanned more than twenty years. [It] reached thousands of victims. . . . Moreover, as many of the victims have pointed out, this is not just a matter of money. The breach of trust was massive. . . . The message must be sent that Mr. Madoff's crimes were extraordinarily evil, and that this kind of irresponsible manipulation of the system is not merely a bloodless financial crime that takes place just on paper. . . . The message must be that in a society governed by the rule of law, Mr. Madoff will get what he deserves.[56]

The judge then asked Madoff to stand. There was a tense silence in the room as everyone present awaited the announcement of the penalty. "It is the judgment of this Court," Chin stated clearly and firmly, "that [you] shall be . . . sentenced to a term of 150 years." Hearing these words, people around the room exhaled loudly, and many began conversing excitedly in husky whispers. Raising his hand to quiet them, the judge added, "I will not impose a fine, as whatever assets Mr. Madoff has [will] be applied to restitution for the victims."[57] Then, as if not wanting to waste any more of the state's or the victims' time, Chin briskly adjourned the hearing.

Bernie Madoff, flanked by prosecutor Lisa Baroni and his defense attorney Ira Sorkin, receives a 150-year sentence in prison from Judge Denny Chin for perpetrating the greatest fraud in Wall Street history.

Lives Fallen Apart

Indeed, Madoff's victims, along with millions of average Americans who had been appalled by his crimes, were overjoyed that he had received the maximum sentence allowed by law. That sense of elation was soon overshadowed by more anger and despair, however.

"It's All Gone!!!"

Of the many victims' statements delivered to the New York district court that dealt with the Madoff case, one of the most emotionally wrenching was that of Barbara Brown, who stated:

> My husband and I had an account for over 30 years with Madoff. We put all our investment savings into this account. [Now] it's all gone!!! We only have the assets in our home, and you know the [housing] market now!! We are struggling and living on social security. . . . My 89-year-old mom and 90-year-old step-dad also had an account with Madoff [and] they are practically destitute . . . and ill, and I can't help them. . . . Please send this person [Madoff] to jail for life!!

Quoted in *USA TODAY*, "Victims' Impact Statements for *U.S. v. Bernard L. Madoff*, June 29, 2009." http://i.usatoday.net/money/_pdfs/09-0616-madoff-victims.pdf.

The sad truth was that most, and in some cases all, of the money each had lost was gone forever. Although the authorities were diligently trying to find caches of Madoff's assets around the world, money that might be divided among his victims, very few such assets had been found. Moreover, experts doubted that very many would be found in the future. Out of the tens of billions of dollars investors had lost, all that was left to be divided was about $1 billion, the total worth of Madoff's houses, boats, personal belongings, and known bank accounts.

For those whose lives Madoff had disrupted and broken, therefore, the tough sentence meted out by the court was their main consolation. Some also noted with some satisfaction that Madoff's own life had recently fallen apart. His sons and most other relatives were also among his victims and had lost money, in some cases nearly all they had. Madoff's aging sister, Sondra, for instance, had invested with him for years and was now almost penniless. As a result, a majority of his relatives and close friends had either disowned him or denounced him in the media.

Most of those close to Madoff also refused to visit him in prison. After his sentencing, he was taken to the federal correctional facility in Butner, North Carolina. Fortunately for him, it is not a maximum security prison housing the most violent, dangerous criminals in the country's penal system. As journalist Steve Fishman described it in a June 2010 *New York* magazine article, the place

> is filled with "soft" prisoners, those who might not survive other institutions. . . . The facility had been planned during a brief period of penal optimism and was designed to humanize the prison experience. The physical space resembles a campus, with landscaped yards and hedges shaped by inmates into giant globes. "There's flowers and trees; you can lay out on the grass and tan," an ex-inmate told me with a laugh. "There's no bars. There are windows." There's a gym, a library, pool tables, a chapel, a volleyball court, and an Indian sweat lodge.[58]

The Butner Federal Correctional Complex in Butner, North Carolina, will be Bernie Madoff's home for the rest of his life.

U.S. DEPT. OF JUSTICE
FEDERAL BUREAU OF PRISONS
PRISON CAMP
BUTNER, NC

A Natural Human Longing

One family member who has visited Madoff a few times in prison is his wife, Ruth. She has publicly said that she still loves him despite the fact that in some ways she has suffered nearly as much as the victims of the Ponzi scheme. The government continues to try to deny her use of any family homes and monies, and she is being sued by various individuals and groups hoping to recoup funds stolen from them by her husband.

Yet though Ruth Madoff has not given up on her husband entirely, their cozy, trusting former relationship no longer exists. In an interview given shortly after his sentencing in 2009, she said that the man with whom she had long shared her life had two sides. Sadly, she admitted, one of those sides turned out to be a stranger:

> My husband was the one [that I and my family] respected and trusted with our lives and our livelihoods. . . . Then there is the other man who stunned us all with his confession and is responsible for this terrible situation in which so many now find themselves. Lives have been upended and futures have been taken away. All those touched by this fraud feel betrayed; disbelieving the nightmare they woke to. I am embarrassed and ashamed. Like everyone else, I feel betrayed and confused. The man who committed this horrible fraud is not the man whom I have known for all these years.[59]

Another person who felt Bernie Madoff was not the person he thought he had known was his son Mark. After the older Madoff's arrest and trial, Mark found it nearly impossible to find work because most employers worried he might have been an accomplice in his father's scheme. Also, many of Bernie Madoff's victims were suing the son, despite his having no connection to that scheme. Perhaps because he felt overwhelmed and hopeless, on December 11, 2010, two years after his father's arrest, Mark Madoff committed suicide in his New York City apartment. Some observers remarked that he had become still another link in Bernie Madoff's long chain of broken trusts.

Thus, a major aspect of the Madoff affair remains the degree to which people can or cannot trust others, even those they think they know extremely well. It turned out that Ruth Madoff could not fully trust the man to whom she had devoted herself for decades. Similarly, Mark and Andrew Madoff could not trust their father, nor could Bernie Madoff's thousands of clients trust the man to whom they had handed their life savings.

Some of those who closely followed the case have stated that these investors should have known better. In this view, when they continued to get glowing reports about their investments month after month, year after year, even when the stock market was down, they should have seen red flags flying every which way. In contrast, other observers point out a desire that almost everyone harbors deep down inside. Namely, people badly want to believe that, sooner or later, they might stumble onto riches or some other extraordinary good fortune. Therefore, Madoff took advantage of a very natural, if largely unrealistic, human longing. As one of his biographers, Erin Arvedlund, phrases it, "If anything, the Madoff scandal transcends [rises above] ethnicity, religion, class, and even international borders, and shows that even the savviest and most intelligent people can be duped into believing something that is too good to be true."[60]

Introduction: A Matter of Trust

1. Quoted in PBS, "The Madoff Affair: Investors' Stories," *Frontline*. www.pbs.org/wgbh/pages/frontline/madoff/investors.
2. Quoted in *Wall Street Journal*, "Plea Allocution of Bernard L. Madoff," Public Resources. http://online.wsj.com/public/resources/documents/20090315madoffall.pdf.
3. Peter Sander, *Madoff: Corruption, Deceit, and the Making of the World's Most Notorious Ponzi Scheme*. Guilford, CT: Lyons, 2009, p. xii.
4. Leon Levy, *The Mind of Wall Street: A Legendary Financier on the Perils of Greed and the Mysteries of the Market*. New York: Perseus, 2002, p. 11.

Chapter 1: Happy Days on Rockaway Beach

5. Quoted in Douglas Feiden, "Bernie Madoff Had a Job Saving Lives, Now He's Killed Dreams," *New York Daily News*, December 21, 2008. www.nydailynews.com/ny_local/queens/2008/12/21/2008-12-21_bernie_madoff_had_a_job_saving_lives_now.html.
6. Sander, *Madoff*, p. 18.
7. Jay Portnoy, "Growing Up with the Ponzi King," *Saratoga Springs (NY) Saratogian*, February 13, 2009. www.saratogian.com/articles/2009/02/13/news/doc49959c85cb664044256888.txt.
8. Portnoy, "Growing Up with the Ponzi King."
9. Quoted in Andrew Kirtzman, *Betrayal: The Life and Lies of Bernie Madoff*. New York: HarperCollins, 2009, p. 22.
10. Quoted in Andrew Kirtzman, *Betrayal*, p. 22.
11. Erin Arvedlund, *Too Good to Be True: The Rise and Fall of Bernie Madoff*. New York: Penguin, 2009, p. 16.
12. Quoted in Arvedlund, *Too Good to Be True*, p. 16.
13. Portnoy, "Growing Up with the Ponzi King."
14. Kirtzman, *Betrayal*, p. 29.
15. Portnoy, "Growing Up with the Ponzi King."

Chapter 2: The Good Bernie Madoff

16. Arvedlund, *Too Good to Be True*, pp. 30–31.
17. Quoted in James Bandler and Nicholas Varchaver, "How Bernie Did It," *Fortune*, April 30, 2009. http://money.cnn .com/2009/04/24/news/newsmakers/madoff.fortune/index.htm? postversion=2009042406.
18. Sander, *Madoff*, pp. 46–47.
19. Bandler and Varchaver, "How Bernie Did It."
20. Kirtzman, *Betrayal*, p. 51.

Chapter 3: The Bad Bernie Madoff

21. Sander, *Madoff*, p. xi.
22. Quoted in Arvedlund, *Too Good to Be True*, p. 28.
23. Arvedlund, *Too Good to Be True*, p. 27.
24. Bandler and Varchaver, "How Bernie Did It."
25. Sander, *Madoff*, pp. 57–58.
26. Harry Markopolos, *No One Would Listen*. New York: Wiley, 2010, pp. 49–50.
27. Bandler and Varchaver, "How Bernie Did It."

Chapter 4: Something Rotten in New York?

28. Markopolos, *No One Would Listen*, p. 132.
29. Quoted in Bandler and Varchaver, "How Bernie Did It."
30. Quoted in Bandler and Varchaver, "How Bernie Did It."
31. Quoted in SEC Madoff Exhibits, "Investigation Closing Narrative, NY-7563, Certain Hedge Fund Trading Practices." www .sec.gov/news/studies/2009/oig-509/exhibit-0389.pdf.
32. Sander, *Madoff*, p. 107.

Chapter 5: His Scheme Exposed at Last

33. Quoted in Brian Ross, *The Madoff Chronicles: Inside the Secret World of Bernie and Ruth*. New York: Hyperion, 2009, p.1.
34. Quoted in Brian Ross, *The Madoff Chronicles: Inside the Secret World of Bernie and Ruth*, p. 3.
35. Markopolos, *No One Would Listen*, p. 38.
36. Quoted in Ross, *The Madoff Chronicles*, pp. 15–16.
37. Quoted in Ross, *The Madoff Chronicles*, p. 20.

38. Quoted in Arvedlund, *Too Good to Be True*, p. 12.
39. Markopolos, *No One Would Listen*, p. 114.
40. Quoted in PBS, "The Madoff Affair."

Chapter 6: Madoff Guilty on All Charges

41. Quoted in *New York Times*, "Bid to Revoke Madoff's Bail Cited His Gifts," January 5, 2009. www.nytimes.com/2009/01/06/business/06madoff.html.
42. Sander, *Madoff*, p. 127.
43. David Segal and Alison L. Cowan, "Madoffs Shared Much; Question Is How Much," *New York Times*, January 14, 2009. www.nytimes.com/2009/01/15/business/15ruth.html.
44. Quoted in U.S. District Court, Southern District of New York, "Madoff Guilty Plea Hearing, March 12, 2009." www.justice.gov/usao/nys/madoff/madoffhearing031209.pdf.
45. Quoted in U.S. District Court, Southern District of New York, "Madoff Guilty Plea Hearing."
46. Quoted in U.S. District Court, Southern District of New York, "Madoff Guilty Plea Hearing."
47. Quoted in U.S. District Court, Southern District of New York, "Madoff Guilty Plea Hearing."
48. Ira Lee Sorkin, "Plea for Leniency for Benard L. Madoff," Scribd, June 22, 2009. www.scribd.com/doc/16699848/Madoff-Letter-Seeking-Leniency.

Chapter 7: A Monster Faces His Victims

49. Quoted in *USATODAY*, "Madoff Sentencing Hearing, June 29, 2009," U.S. District Court, Southern District of New York. www.usatoday.com/money/_pdfs/madoff-sentencing-transcript.pdf.
50. Quoted in *USA TODAY*, "Victims' Impact Statements for *U.S. v. Bernard L. Madoff*, June 29, 2009." http://i.usatoday.net/money/_pdfs/09-0616-madoff-victims.pdf.
51. Quoted in *USA TODAY*, "Victims' Impact Statements."
52. Quoted in *USA TODAY*, "Victims' Impact Statements."
53. Quoted in *USATODAY*, "Madoff Sentencing Hearing."
54. Quoted in *USATODAY*, "Madoff Sentencing Hearing."
55. Quoted in *USATODAY*, "Madoff Sentencing Hearing."

56. Quoted in *USATODAY*, "Madoff Sentencing Hearing"
57. Quoted in *USATODAY*, "Madoff Sentencing Hearing."
58. Steve Fishman, "Bernie Madoff, Free at Last," *New York*, June 6, 2010. http://nymag.com/news/crimelaw/66 468.
59. *Wall Street Journal*, "Ruth Madoff Issues Statement Regarding Husband's Fraud," June 29, 2009. http://online.wsj.com/article/SB124629343582068785.html.
60. Arvedlund, *Too Good to Be True*, p. 273.

Important Dates

1920
Ambitious con man Charles Ponzi becomes famous when his huge financial pyramid scheme collapses and he is arrested for fraud.

1929
The U.S. stock market crashes, sending the country and most of the world into a long financial depression.

1938
On April 29, Bernard L. Madoff is born in the New York City borough of Queens.

1941–1945
The United States participates in World War II.

1956
Madoff graduates from Far Rockaway High School in southern Queens.

1959
Madoff marries his high school sweetheart Ruth Alpern.

1960
John F. Kennedy is elected president of the United States; Madoff starts a small-scale stock-trading business.

1964–1965
The U.S. Congress passes a series of sweeping bills granting civil rights to blacks and other minorities.

1971
Emergence of the NASDAQ, an electronic stock-trading market pioneered by a group of eager young traders, including Madoff.

1973
Madoff's stock-trading business makes a profit of more than $1 million.

1981
The Madoffs purchase a $3 million house in the Hamptons on Long Island.

1984
With the stock market and other financial institutions making big profits, Ronald Reagan is elected to a second term as U.S. president.

1992
Some of Madoff's associates are investigated by the Securities and Exchange Commission for wrongdoing, but his ongoing secret investment scam escapes detection.

1994
Madoff and his wife buy a mansion in Palm Beach, Florida.

2000
George W. Bush is elected president of the United States; Madoff's scam reaches a total of about $7 billion worth of investments.

2001
Terrorists destroy the World Trade Center Towers in New York City, sending a ripple of fear through U.S. financial markets.

2005–2006
Another Securities and Exchange Commission investigation fails to uncover Madoff's fraud.

2008
Madoff's scam collapses; on December 11, FBI agents arrest him at his apartment in Manhattan; his bail is set for $10 million.

2009
On March 12, Madoff pleads guilty to financial fraud and other charges in a New York district court; on June 29, he is sentenced to serve 150 years in prison.

Books

Erin Arvedlund, *Too Good to Be True: The Rise and Fall of Bernie Madoff*. New York: Penguin, 2009. A well-researched, comprehensive overview of Madoff's life, crimes, and downfall.

Andrew Kirtzman, *Betrayal: The Life and Lies of Bernie Madoff*. New York: HarperCollins, 2009. One of the better recent biographies of Madoff.

Leon Levy, *The Mind of Wall Street: A Legendary Financier on the Perils of Greed and the Mysteries of the Market*. New York: Perseus, 2002. Those interested in the stock market and its complexities will find this a revealing and riveting read.

Harry Markopolos, *No One Would Listen*. New York: Wiley, 2010. Markopolos, a financial analyst who investigated Madoff for years, explains how he and his associates concluded Madoff was running the world's largest Ponzi scheme.

Brian Ross, *The Madoff Chronicles: Inside the Secret World of Bernie and Ruth*. New York: Hyperion, 2009. The reputable ABC reporter delivers a blow-by-blow description of the unraveling of Madoff's financial empire.

Peter Sander, *Madoff: Corruption, Deceit, and the Making of the World's Most Notorious Ponzi Scheme*. Guilford, CT: Lyons, 2009. A well-written general overview of Madoff's life, focusing mainly on the financial mechanics of the Wall Street world in which Madoff operated for decades.

Web Sites

Frontline: "The Madoff Affair" (www.pbs.org/wgbh/pages/frontline/madoff). An excellent examination of Madoff and his financial scam, with several statements by his victims.

How Stuff Works: How the NASDAQ Stock Exchange Works (http://money.howstuffworks.com). Explains how the electronic stock market that Bernie Madoff headed on several occasions works.

Times **Topics: "Ponzi Schemes"** (http://topics.nytimes.com/topics/reference/timestopics/subjects/f/frauds_and_swindling/ponzi_schemes/index.html). Explains the workings of a Ponzi scheme, the method Madoff used to bilk his clients; includes a photo and brief bio of one of its originators, Charles Ponzi.

U.S. Department of Justice: *United States* **v.** *Bernard L. Madoff and Related Cases* (www.justice.gov/usao/nys/madoff.html). A collection of official court documents relating to the Madoff case.

Picture Credits

Cover: Stephen Chermin/Getty Images
Daniel Acker/Bloomberg/Getty Images, 20
AP Images, 38
AP Images/Mary Altaffer, 77
AP Images/Gerry Broome, 81
AP Images/Christine Cornell, 70
AP Images/Jennifer Graylock, 35
AP Images/McMullan Co/Sipa, 7
AP Images/David J. Phillip, 57
AP Images/Nick Ut, 55
AP Images/Seth Wenig, 74
© Bettmann/Corbis, 39
Boston Globe/Joanne Rathe/Landov, 48
Christine Cornell/AFP/Getty Images, 66
Stephane DannaAFP/Getty Images, 43
Gino Domenico/Bloomberg News/Getty Images, 42
Don Emmert/AFP/Getty Images, 50, 60
Andrew Harrer/Bloomberg/Getty Images, 18, 33
Jin Lee/Bloomberg/Getty Images, 63
New York Daily News/Getty Images, 10, 53
Ezio Petersen/UPI/Landov, 25
Spencer Platt/Getty Images, 49
Reuters/Shepard/Landov, 79
Frances M. Roberts/Getty Images, 29
Sam Shere/Time Life Pictures/Getty Images, 14

Historian and award-winning writer Don Nardo has published many volumes of both single and multiple biography, among his subjects Aristotle, Confucius, Julius Caesar, Cleopatra, Tycho Brahe, Ivan the Terrible, Thomas Jefferson, Charles Darwin, Andrew Johnson, H.G. Wells, Queen Victoria, Franklin D. Roosevelt, and Adolf Hitler. Nardo also writes screenplays and teleplays and composes music. He resides in Massachusetts with his wife, Christine.